An Economic Perspective on the Southwest: Defining the Decade

An Economic Perspective on the Southwest: Defining the Decade

Proceedings of the 1990 Conference on the Southwest Economy Sponsored by the Federal Reserve Bank of Dallas

Edited by
Gerald P. O'Driscoll, Jr.
Stephen P. A. Brown
The Federal Reserve Bank of Dallas

KLUWER ACADEMIC PUBLISHERS
Boston/Dordrecht/London

Distributors for North America:
Kluwer Academic Publishers
101 Philip Drive
Assinippi Park
Norwell, Massachusetts 02061 USA

Distributors for all other countries:
Kluwer Academic Publishers Group
Distribution Centre
Post Office Box 322
3300 AH Dordrecht, THE NETHERLANDS

Library of Congress Cataloging-in-Publication Data
Conference on the Southwest Economy (1990 : Dallas, Tex.)
An economic perspective on the Southwest : defining the decade : proceedings of the 1990 Conference on the Southwest Economy / sponsored by the Federal Reserve Bank of Dallas ; edited by Gerald P. O'Driscoll, Jr., Stephen P. A. Brown.
p. cm.
Includes bibliographical references.
ISBN 0-7923-9221-3
1. Southwestern States--Economic conditions--Congresses. 2. International economic relations--Congresses. 3. Economic history--1971- --Congresses. I. O'Driscoll, Gerald P. II. Brown, Stephen P. A. (Stephen Paul Adolph), 1948- . III. Federal Reserve Bank of Dallas. IV. Title.
HC107.A165 1990
330.978'033--dc20 91-31513
CIP

Printed on acid-free paper.

Printed in the United States of America

Contents

Preface

As the Southwest entered the 1990s, the region was starting to regain the economic momentum it lost in the mid-1980s. Texas, Louisiana and New Mexico—the states of the Eleventh District of the Federal Reserve System—were struggling to develop a more diversified economy and new, perhaps international, markets to achieve the growth that would lead them out of recession and into recovery.

At the same time, other parts of the nation had begun to feel the impact of a broader recession that coincided with escalating hostilities in the Persian Gulf. War had not yet started, and the world waited and watched to see how high oil prices would soar and how long the downturn would persist. Such was the economic climate November 15–16, 1990, when more than 300 participants met in Dallas, Texas, for the Federal Reserve Bank of Dallas' third annual conference on the Southwest economy, "Defining the Decade."

These proceedings demonstrate our desire to preserve and promote the ideas expressed at the conference. This written account serves as a snapshot, a reminder of where we were, what we were thinking, during those two days in the fall of 1990. Already we know the outcome of the Persian Gulf war, but other events taking shape in late 1990 will take years to unfold—the conversion of Eastern Europe to a market economy, which Federal Reserve Chairman Alan Greenspan described in the keynote address; the implementation of a free trade agreement between the United States and Mexico, which James R. Markusen discussed; and—closer to home—economic development in the region, such as Fort Worth's Alliance Airport, which developer Ross Perot, Jr., discussed.

The organization of these proceedings reflects the conference format. Part One, Defining the Decade, consists of speeches delivered at general sessions: Federal Reserve Chairman Greenspan's keynote address and the kickoff speech by Admiral Bobby Inman, USN (retired).

Part Two, The Changing International Marketplace, provides a look at

Germany as a marketplace, prospects for a U.S.–Mexico free trade agreement and trends in Japanese money flows.

Part Three, Investing in the Future, covers strategies for business development, the shortfall in public investment and a look at public and private finance. The part also includes the address by Ross Perot, Jr.

Part Four, Perspectives on the Energy Market, presents several views on oil prices, markets, exploration and alternatives in the 1990s.

Part Five, The Future of the Southwest Economy, presents Dallas Fed Senior Vice President Harvey Rosenblum's economic outlook for the Southwest and excerpts from a panel discussion by five Southwest leaders. Panelists were Dan Morales, who was elected Texas attorney general in November 1990; Houston Mayor Kathryn Whitmire; Dallas Fed economist Bill Gruben; Dallas attorney Tom Luce, who campaigned for governor in Texas in 1990; and Diana Natalicio, president of the University of Texas at El Paso.

This success of this conference reflects the contributions of many individuals. We wish to thank Gene Autry, Tara Barrett, Laura J. Bell, Robert H. Boykin, Susan August Brown, Kim Ernst, Helen Holcomb, Linda Hunter, Michael Levy, Tad Lichtenauer, Bill Long, Kurt Phippen, Harvey Rosenblum, Paula Tucker, Sammie Vaught, William H. Wallace and the speakers, who helped make this conference one of the best. We also wish to thank our editorial staff, Rhonda Harris, Diana Palmer and Virginia Rogers, for their help in making this volume possible.

Gerald P. O'Driscoll, Jr.
Stephen P.A. Brown

About the Contributors

ROBERT H. BOYKIN served as president and chief executive officer of the Federal Reserve Bank of Dallas from 1981 until January 1991. A native of West Texas, he holds B.B.A. and J.D. degrees from the University of Texas at Austin and is a graduate of the School of Banking of the South at Louisiana State University. He currently serves as a member of the Advisory Council for the School of Management and Administration for the University of Texas at Dallas as well as an advisory member of the Dallas Citizens Council. Boykin joined the Dallas Fed in 1953 as an attorney. Before his election to president, he served as first vice president and chief operating officer.

STEPHEN P.A. BROWN is assistant vice president and senior economist at the Federal Reserve Bank of Dallas. In this position, he is responsible for managing the energy and regional economics section of the Research Department and two Bank publications, *Economic Review* and *Southwest Economy*. He is the author of numerous articles on business conditions and economic policy. His research focuses on the Southwest economy and energy issues. His work has received national and international attention from the academic community and such publications as *The Economist*, the *New York Times* and *Time* magazine. He holds a bachelor's degree in economics from California Polytechnic State University and a master's degree and doctorate in economics from the University of Maryland. Brown joined the Dallas Fed in 1981, after working as an energy economist for Brookhaven National Laboratory and after teaching economics at several universities.

DAN W. COOK, III, has been a general partner for Goldman, Sachs & Co. since 1977 and was chairman of the Texas Select Committee on Tax Equity. He serves on the executive committee to the Advisory Board to the Center for the Study of Financial Institutions and Markets at the Edwin L. Cox School of Business at

Southern Methodist University. Cook also serves as a member of the Dallas Citizens Council and as a trustee for Southwestern Medical Foundation. He received his bachelor's degree from Stanford University and a master's degree from the Harvard Graduate School of Business Administration.

RICHARD W. FISHER is managing partner of Fisher Capital Management, a firm that manages more than $300 million in globally diversified discretionary portfolios for private investors. Previously, he was senior manager of the private banking firm of Brown Brothers Harriman & Co. From 1977 to 1979, Fisher was executive assistant to the Secretary of the Treasury of the United States. In this capacity, he served as the secretary's chief of staff for international affairs and interacted with the heads of state and finance ministers of Europe, Latin America, the Far East and the Middle East. He was a member of a team that negotiated the normalization of trade with the People's Republic of China, and he served as assistant to President Jimmy Carter at the Tokyo Summit and as an adviser at the Bonn Economic Summit. Fisher graduated with honors from Harvard University with a bachelor's degree in economics, and he has a master's degree in business administration from Stanford University.

EDWARD M. GRAMLICH is professor of economics and public policy at the University of Michigan. He has chaired the economics department there and is currently director of its Institute for Public Policy Studies. He also has served as a staff member at the Federal Reserve Board of Governors, as director of the Policy Research Division at the Office of Economic Opportunity, as a senior fellow at the Brookings Institution, and as both deputy director and acting director of the Congressional Budget Office. He is an author of both books and articles on budget policy, macroeconomics, fiscal federalism and income redistribution. He holds a doctorate in economics from Yale University.

ALAN GREENSPAN was sworn in on August 11, 1987, as chairman of the Board of Governors of the Federal Reserve System. In this capacity, he also serves as chairman of the Federal Open Market Committee, the System's principal monetary policy-making body. A native of New York City, Greenspan holds bachelor's, master's and doctoral degrees in economics from New York University. Before his appointment as chairman, Greenspan was chairman and president of Townsend–Greenspan & Co. Inc., an economic consulting firm in New York City. From 1974 to 1977, he served as chairman of the President's Council of Economic Advisers under President Gerald Ford and as chairman of the National Commission on Social Security Reform from 1981 to 1983. In addition, he has served as a member of President Ronald Reagan's Economic Policy Advisory Board, a member of *Time* magazine's board of economists, senior adviser to the Brookings Panel on Economic Activity and a consultant to the Congressional Budget Office.

WILLIAM C. GRUBEN is a senior economist and policy adviser at the Federal Reserve Bank of Dallas and an adjunct professor of economics at Southern Methodist University. He has written extensively on regional economic growth and regional business cycles, public finance and state and local government fiscal policy, labor economics, international finance and the construction industry. He holds a doctorate in economics from the University of Texas at Austin. He is a member of the board of advisors of the University of Texas Bureau of Business Research and *Dallas Morning News* Board of Economists.

HILLARD G. HUNTINGTON is the executive director of the Energy Modeling Forum at Stanford University. In this position, he conducts studies to improve the use and usefulness of energy models for business planning and policy analysis. He has coordinated major studies evaluating models for international oil markets, macroeconomic forecasting and North American natural gas markets. His work in professional journals and books has focused principally on energy markets and policy, energy demand and energy–economy interactions. Before accepting his position at Stanford, Huntington was the director of the Washington Energy Office for Data Resources Inc. He was a staff economist for the Federal Energy Administration and a visiting research associate for the Institute for Development Studies at the University of Nairobi in Kenya. He received his bachelor's degree from Cornell University and his doctorate in economics from the State University of New York.

ADMIRAL BOBBY R. INMAN, USN (retired), is an investor and former chairman of the board of the Federal Reserve Bank of Dallas. His career with naval intelligence spanned two decades, and he retired with the permanent rank of admiral in 1982. Between 1974 and 1982, Inman served as director of naval intelligence, director of the National Security Agency and deputy director of the Central Intelligence Agency. From 1983 through 1986, he served as chairman and chief executive officer of the Microelectronics and Computer Technology Corp. (MCC) in Austin, Texas. Then he served as chairman, president and chief executive officer of Westmark Systems Inc., a privately owned electronics industry holding company.

ISAAC C. KERRIDGE, JR., is corporate vice president of Baker Hughes Inc., a major oil-field service company headquartered in Houston. He was employed by

Rice University and the Prudential Insurance Co. before accepting a position at Hughes Tool Co. in 1956. Hughes Tool and Baker International Corp. merged in April 1987 to form Baker Hughes Inc. Kerridge is a member of the International Association of Energy Economists, the National Association of Business Economists and the Independent Petroleum Association of America. He received his bachelor's and master's degrees from the University of Texas at Austin.

EDWARD N. KRAPELS is the founder and president of Energy Security Analysis Inc. He is an internationally recognized expert on the world petroleum market. Krapels also is the executive director of Petroleum Economics Ltd. of London and president of PEL North America. Energy Security Analysis has become well-known for STOCKWATCH, an influential oil market analysis service. His companies provide medium- and long-term oil and energy supply, demand and price forecasts, as well as detailed analyses of political developments in OPEC countries and energy and environmental policy developments in industrial and developing countries. Krapels received his bachelor's degree from the University of North Carolina at Chapel Hill, his master's degree from the University of Chicago and his doctorate from the School of Advanced International Studies of the Johns Hopkins University.

MICHAEL R. LEVY is publisher of *Texas Monthly* and chairman and president of the magazine's parent company, Mediatex Communications Corp. Levy is a native of Dallas and a graduate of the Wharton School at the University of Pennsylvania and the University of Texas School of Law. Before founding *Texas Monthly* in 1973, Levy worked for United Press International and *Philadelphia Magazine.* He is a member of the State Bar of Texas and the Young Presidents' Organization. He is on the board of directors of the Magazine Publishers of America. In addition, he serves on the board of visitors for the University of Texas M. D. Anderson Cancer Center and the University of Texas School of Law.

TOM LUCE founded the Dallas law firm of Hughes and Luce in 1973 with four partners. In 1990, he ran for the Republican nomination for governor of Texas. Although he did not receive the nomination, he was endorsed statewide by 15 newspapers, which cited his integrity and experience in dealing with state and national issues. He has served the state of Texas in various capacities, including chairman of the Texas National Research Laboratory Commission, the agency responsible for Texas' participation in the Superconducting Super Collider Laboratory, and chief of staff of the Texas Select Committee on Public Education, helping to draft sweeping changes to Texas' public education system. He received his bachelor's and law degrees from Southern Methodist University.

JAMES R. MARKUSEN is a professor of economics at the University of Colorado at Boulder. After earning his undergraduate degree and doctorate in economics from Boston College, Markusen joined the faculty of the University of Western Ontario in Canada. His primary research interest is international trade, particularly the economics of multinational corporations. Recently, he began research on the possible effects of a free trade agreement between Mexico and the United States. He is the author of several books and serves as a lecturer around the world. In addition to his teaching and research activities, he is a research associate for the National Bureau of Economic Research.

DAN MORALES was elected attorney general of Texas in November 1990. He served in Texas' House of Representatives from 1986 to 1990. Morales, a native of San Antonio, is an honors graduate of Trinity University and Harvard Law School. In 1982, he gave up his private law practice to become a Bexar County assistant district attorney. His experiences as a prosecutor spurred him to run for public office. He has been honored for his work in the Texas Legislature, including being named one of the "Seven Best Legislators" of 1987 by the *Dallas Morning News*.

DIANA NATALICIO is the president of the University of Texas at El Paso. She received her bachelor's degree in Spanish, *summa cum laude*, from St. Louis University, a master's degree in Portuguese and a doctorate in linguistics from the University of Texas at Austin. She was a Fulbright scholar in Rio de Janeiro, Brazil, and a visiting scholar in Lisbon, Portugal. After serving as a research associate at the Center for Communication Research at the University of Texas at Austin, Natalicio joined the faculty of the University of Texas at El Paso in 1971. In addition to her teaching responsibilities, she has served the University in numerous administrative capacities, including dean of liberal arts and vice president for academic affairs.

GERALD P. O'DRISCOLL, JR., is vice president at the Federal Reserve Bank of Dallas. He is an adviser on monetary policy to the president of the Dallas Fed. He received his master's degree and doctorate in economics from the University of California at Los Angeles and has served as a professor of economics for several universities. He has written articles and papers on monetary economics, industrial organization, and law and economics. He is also the author of several books, the most recent being the internationally recognized *Economics of Time and Ignorance*, co-written with Mario J. Rizzo.

ROSS PEROT, JR., directs the real estate division of The Perot Group in Dallas. A native of Dallas, Perot received a bachelor of business administration degree from Vanderbilt University in 1981. In September 1982, he completed the first flight around the world in a helicopter. Flying more than 26,000 miles in less than 30 days, he crossed 26 countries and 21 seas and oceans. His helicopter, *The Spirit of Texas*, is currently on display in the Smithsonian Institution's Air and Space Museum. His largest project for The Perot Group involves three interrelated endeavors. The first is a 3,000-acre, master-planned business park, called Alliance, surrounding Fort Worth Alliance Airport, which is the first airport to be conceived and built for the industrial user. The second is a mixed-use residential development encompassing 3,500 acres south of Alliance Airport. The third is a project in conjunction with the State Highway Department to construct an 18-mile freeway connecting D/FW Airport and Alliance Airport.

HARVEY ROSENBLUM is senior vice president and director of research for the Federal Reserve Bank of Dallas. In this capacity, he serves as the chief economic policy adviser to the Bank's president and as an associate economist for the Federal Open Market Committee. In addition to his advisory duties regarding the formulation of monetary, regulatory and regional economic policies, his current research interests center on banking structure and regulation, deposit insurance reform and monetary policy. Before joining the Dallas Fed in 1985, Rosenblum was the vice president and associate director of research for the Federal Reserve Bank of Chicago. In addition to his work for the Federal Reserve, Rosenblum also serves as a visiting professor of finance and economics at Southern Methodist University.

KEREN K. WARE is program manager of the Office of Advanced Technology in the Business Development Division of the Texas Department of Commerce. Ware previously served as research analyst and chief clerk of the Texas House of Representatives' Science and Technology Committee. In the spring of 1988, she took a leave of absence from the committee and traveled extensively through Asia and Australia to meet with more than 80 representatives of educational institutions, technology policy companies and high-tech businesses in six countries. She chairs the executive board of the Texas Alliance for Science, Technology, and Mathematics Education and is on the board of the Texas Computer Industry Council. She also is a member of the Technology Industry Legislative Task Force and the Texas Women's Political Caucus. Ware received her bachelor's degree in chemistry from Harvard University.

CHRISTIAN WATRIN has been a professor of economics at the University of Cologne since 1971. During this time, he also served as a member and vice chairman of the Advisory Council to the Federal Ministry of Economic Affairs. Currently, he is chairman of that organization and is also the managing director of the Institute for Economic Policy at the University of Cologne. Watrin has served as a member and chairman of the board at the Federal Institute for East European and International Studies.

KATHRYN J. WHITMIRE was inaugurated as mayor of Houston in 1982. She began her fifth term in 1990. Before serving as mayor, she was elected city controller in 1977 and was re-elected to that post in 1979. A Houston native, Whitmire is a certified public accountant, and she was associated with a national CPA firm in Houston for eight years. She earned both her undergraduate and graduate degrees from the University of Houston. Whitmire is the immediate past president of the U.S. Conference of Mayors, a past president of the Texas Municipal League and a member of the board of directors of the Greater Houston Partnership.

PART ONE

Defining the Decade

"A society cannot be organized around a principle by which individuals deal with one another in a way they perceive, at root, to be unethical....A major precondition to the East's transition to a market system will be its philosophical transformation."

—Alan Greenspan

"As I look at this decade, there are more uncertainties than at any time in my adult life....Many things that were certainties all my adult life are now changing."

—Admiral Bobby R. Inman

The Changing International Marketplace

Alan Greenspan

What I would like to focus on is something that has slipped off the front pages, largely because the media focuses on what is most important at any particular time. Clearly, at the moment the real thrust is on the Middle East, oil prices, the possibilities of war and the whole series of related issues. But it is almost too soon to be distracted from what could be the most important event in the second half of the 20th century—the transition of the centrally planned economies of the Soviet Union and its former Eastern European satellites to market systems.

A Four-Decade Experiment

When Churchill went to Fulton, Missouri, in 1946 and described the Iron Curtain coming down across Central Europe, he in a sense was describing what turned out to be a most extraordinary and unprecedented experiment in economic theory. No one had planned it, and it was inadvertent in all respects. But what we, in effect, saw resulting between the end of World War II and 1989 was a four-decade experiment in the two fundamental competitive theories of social and economic organization. What evolved in the East on one side of the Iron Curtain and in the West on the opposite side was essentially as close to a laboratory experiment that one could have in the social sciences.

When I was a student, the conventional wisdom was that socialism was clearly the most efficient means of organizing economies. A common view held that capitalism offered certain elements of efficiency but probably could not stand up as a fundamental competitive force against a centrally planned economy.

In 1989, we stripped away the Iron Curtain with the figuratively important destruction of the Berlin Wall. We saw the results of what for 40 years was essentially an experiment in which we attempted to hold constant cultures, different types of peoples, education and technology. The Iron Curtain had formed a line that in many respects separated towns that were continuous, dividing people who were closely related. One would have thought that the final results would have been ambiguous. They were not.

The results were unequivocal. Not even the slightest element of uncertainty remained in their evaluation. What we saw coming out of the rubble of World War II were market economies in Western Europe that flourished, while the centrally planned economies appeared to be caught in a time warp of the late 1940s and the 1950s. It is as though time stood still in Eastern Europe.

Crossing the Berlin Wall into East Berlin and, somewhat earlier, seeing parts of Eastern Europe was like walking into history. Worse, what one saw were heavily polluted environments and extraordinarily inefficient use of energy and materials. Most important, the standard of living on the other side of this experimental Iron Curtain was much lower than we in the West had imagined. The conventional wisdom within U.S. intelligence organizations was that East Germany was the star of Eastern Europe, and its standard of living was almost at the level of West Germany. In the official figures, GNP per capita was a bit lower than in West Germany, but not dramatically so. Over the past year as we took a close look at what was going on there—received real data and looked at the infrastructure and the way the system was functioning—it became very clear that our previous assessments were way off.

Real GNP in the East and in the West: A Difficult Comparison

One of the major reasons we made that mistake was because we were looking at our conventional GNP measures. When we endeavor to measure the difference between the standards of living in France and Belgium, for example, we look at both countries' per capita GNP and come up with a pretty good idea as to what the balance sheets look like. But when we look at market-economy data from the West, we are measuring apples and apples. The same is not true when we look at this extraordinary set of data in Eastern Europe.

It is not altogether irrelevant that Eastern Europe has lived in a time warp. In an odd way, what we are doing when we measure their GNPs is adding up what the GNP would look like if we as statisticians went back into 1949 and 1950. The trouble with doing that is if we in the West were to look at the GNPs that we produced in 1949 and 1950, we would find that in today's environment, half of it could not be sold because consumers would not accept the quality or level of technology embodied in those old goods. Nonetheless, we could still add it up and get a big number.

It became obvious that something was wrong when the economies of East and West Germany were joined and we found that East Germans would not buy East German yogurt. Now, there is no chemical difference between West German yogurt and East German yogurt. It was startling to find that the packaging of the West German product is what took the market away from East Germany. There is no technology in that; there is no quality difference. Imagine what the issue is when you begin to look at quality.

You cannot add up the GNP engendered by the production of motor vehicles in East Germany and match it against West Germany because, when confronted with a market, no one will buy the East German vehicles. Therefore, when you try to calculate Eastern Europe's real GNP, you not only have to adjust for the differences in the actual levels of goods and services produced but also the quality of those goods and whether they are viable in a competitive world market, as indeed—of necessity—goods are in the West. When you make those adjustments, what you find in bringing the economies of Eastern Europe forward from 1950 to 1990 is a substantial "marking down" in our estimates of their standard of living and capability of producing.

Now, one can argue that a 1950 refrigerator is better than none at all, and that there is some value there. When push comes to shove, there is value there, except in a competitive environment. So, one does not exactly know what to say the standard of living is, except that it is substantially less than any of us in the West had contemplated before the Berlin Wall came down.

It did not take a panel of economic scientists to determine which form of economic organization prevailed in the appropriate manner. It was not necessary. Mikhail Gorbachev, by indicating early on the need for *perestroika*, essentially said, "Our economy needs restructuring."

The Uncharted Course from Central Planning to a Market Economy

This outcome was also obvious in the extraordinary move of all the centrally planned economies toward a market system in the past several years. The trouble, as we are learning, is that the desirability of moving to a market economy is one thing; doing it is another. A significant majority opinion, if not a consensus, in Eastern Europe is that, "Centrally planned economies have failed; market systems work and, therefore, that is where we want to go." The difficulty is that we have never seen a transition from a centrally planned economy to a market economy in any major industrial country. We have no real judgment as to the actual mechanism through which such a change is best implemented. And what we are seeing is a series of approaches, none of which has demonstrated complete success.

Obviously, the Poles have gone cold turkey toward a market economy.

They, in effect, said, "We don't have the luxury of doing it in slow motion." Without question, Poland has shown some very significant improvement. But the country has a long way to go, and how the ultimate resolution will occur is not yet clear.

Different countries in Eastern Europe are in differing stages of transition and have differing ideas of how to move toward a market economy. We do not yet see any real, unquestioned successes, and we do not yet see the integrations that inevitably are going to occur. We know, though, that whatever happens, East Germany is being forced into the market structure of West Germany. And it is only a matter of time before the issue of East Germany's transition gets resolved one way or another. And in many respects, I would probably say much the same about Eastern Europe as well.

The Crucial Role of Competition

The conclusion of this economic experiment is unequivocal. But it is not clear just yet why central planning—a concept that evolved for 100 years—failed so abysmally in practice. My suspicion is that, when all the Ph.D. theses are written, what will differentiate the two types of systems will be competition. This notion is very simple, but clearly competition is the driving force for progress in the West. And we find a complete lack of competition, by construction, in the East. Indeed, the word *competition* in socialist dogma, in any centrally planned dogma, is usually perceived to be destructive, socially undesirable and, in some theses, marginally immoral. As a result, you see constructed in all centrally planned economies an extraordinary set of state monopolies.

Whereas we in the West, by design, foster multiple competitors for any particular product, in centrally planned economies, a surprisingly large number of major products are produced by one producer, usually in one plant. And these producers are, by design, state monopolies. This distinction of economic organization, this competition, is what happens to differentiate the two systems. (Of course, competition has a lot of other collateral issues associated with it, not the least of which is the importance of economic freedom.)

In the West, competition is something we all appreciate conceptually. And for those of us schooled in market economics, it is the fundamental issue. But we do not necessarily like competition. A professor of economics, for example, does not like some smart-alecky kid competing with him by writing papers. Or if you own a grocery store on the corner and some smart-alecky kid opens another store across the street, you hate it! But it makes you work harder. The professor thinks a little more, writes a little better, does his work a little better and is better for it. And so is the grocery store owner.

The market system works. It works essentially because competition—granted, the nature of the human species—induces individuals to increased effort, to more productive effort. And when you set up a society that is competitive, you would think—and indeed we find—that we get far more material goods and services. In fact, we get much more than materials and services; we get an intellectual product that is vastly superior to that in a society in which competition is perceived to be, at least at root, unethical, undesirable, unimplementable.

In a secondary sense, by looking at our financial institutions we can see the forces of competition working their way through these two different types of systems. It is no accident that in the West we have extraordinarily complex financial instruments, financial institutions—a whole structure of prices and means to assist in the allocation of goods and services. In the centrally planned economies, similar institutions do not exist.

In fact, the greater the centrally planned aspect of an economy, the less you need financial institutions. You do not need commercial banks. You do not need finance companies, you do not need stock exchanges, you do not need bond markets or the whole list of institutions that we take for granted.

A centrally planned economy also lacks the types of peripheral economic services that assist in creating the goods and services that expand living standards in the West. Accounting, for example, has a different purpose in a centrally planned economy than in the West. In the West, we set up our accounts and depreciate our capital investments. If we buy a computer or build a plant, we depreciate it. We write it off in part, according to our view as to its economic life. What we mean by *economic life* is the period over which that facility will produce or assist in the production of goods and services that serve markets and thus help fulfill the value preferences of a society. We have learned through experience how long it takes to write off something. And when we write it off, we usually scrap whatever it is, saying, "It is no longer economical; it is no longer producing."

No such concept exists in a centrally planned economy. Notions such as *relative value*, *economic*, *non-economic*, *profit* and *non-profit* do not exist. In centrally planned economies, no one writes off capital goods. And the reason they do not is that centrally planned economies, lacking a value system derived from the preferences of the individuals who live in the society, will keep equipment in use as long as it mechanically functions.

If you cross the old Iron Curtain, what you will find are World War II tractors on the farms. The tractors still work; keep patching them up and they will work. They are grossly inefficient, and even letting those things run is an extraordinary misuse of resources. For example, I recall that when I was very young

Czechoslovakia was presumed to be in the forefront of certain elements of technology in the world. And then the Iron Curtain came down for 40-odd years, then the Iron Curtain came back up, and what we saw was the same Czechoslovakia that existed 40 and 50 years ago. And the high-tech of 40 or 50 years ago is still there, but it is no longer high technology.

An Extraordinary, Malfunctioning System

The system does not allow the valuative process. It does not allow competitive forces to function. And when you look at how this difference affects the infrastructure, how goods move from one place to another and how the system interacts, what you get is this extraordinary, malfunctioning system. The Soviet Union, for example, by not replacing equipment in the way we replace it in the West, gets periodic breakdowns in the transportation system, which—remember—is a monopoly. Any breakdown in the transportation system means the whole system is down. Hence, our estimate that 30 percent to 40 percent of the grain produced in the Soviet Union never comes to markets is no accident.

The signs of these problems are becoming so evident that it is very difficult to figure out how in the world the outcome could have been otherwise. And if you begin to look at the underlying theory of central planning versus markets, the reason the experiment we have been through turned out as it did becomes, I think, pretty clear.

The organizing principle of central planning at the extreme—in its purest form, which has never been implemented because it could not be implemented—dictates that you have no money because money is unnecessary. You do not need a financial system. All you basically need is a list of products that some hierarchy in the society decides is of value to produce. And once you have that list of products—so many pairs of shoes, so many men's suits of size X and so many cars—the task becomes an engineering determination of the materials you need to produce that package of goods. In most recent economic evaluations, we say that this process requires an input–output system. That is, a system that tells you how much of different materials you need to produce a certain bill of goods. And indeed, that is precisely what the central planning systems tried to do, in theory.

That system has associated with it no money but ration coupons, which people then use to get back goods. It is a sort of barter system in principle. That sort of system obviously could never work.

Indeed, after 1917 in the early stages of the Soviet Union's moving into a non-capitalist economic system, there was a good deal of discussion of having a no-money state. Money was considered to be the root of all evil, and one should extirpate it as a mechanism to cleanse the society. They could not do that, obviously, and they could not do away with the markets, even in their most rudimentary forms. As a consequence, what they ended up with was very simple money systems. For example, the Soviet Union, until very recently, had only a single bank, which comprised both central bank and commercial bank functions. Other financial institutions did not exist. Money serves an extremely limited purpose in that type of system.

In one sense, that type of system probably appears to work and indeed works, in part, if you are dealing with a military production requirement. What needs to be produced is determined, in the Soviet system, by how many SS-20s or MiG-29s are deemed necessary. Once you determine, for example, the wing structure of a MiG-29 and its attrition, you will figure out basically what its production cycle is. Then you determine the underlying materials and patterns that must be supplied to the assembly plants under a specific schedule. Indeed, our controlled-materials plan during World War II was not significantly different from that type of system. It does not work well; it works inefficiently, but it works in part. We turned out 50,000 planes a year at the peak of World War II. And the system works in part in the Soviet Union.

For example, it is very clear that the Soviet military production system is far superior historically to anything the Soviets produced in their civilian sector. They have separated the types of factories that they have had. Some factories produced primarily military products, with a limited amount of consumer goods. These factories got the skilled workers, skilled technicians, engineers and the like. Other factories produced strictly consumer goods and, having no market competition, were predictably quite shabby and inefficiently put together. In fact, sophisticated Soviet consumers figured out what was produced where and came to expect goods produced at military factories to be of much higher quality than those produced at non-military factories.

The problem, of course, is that we are not in a military-producing system. We are not in a system in which a certain hierarchy, a small group of individuals, determines for a society what the bill of goods demanded by that society should be.

A market society basically is constructed on the presumption that each individual—producers and consumers—in the society has a whole series of preferences. And without going into detail, it is very easy to demonstrate that if each individual has a series of preferences and they meet in a free market, markets will evolve a system of production and prices and wages, which—as we like to say in economics—is *cleared*, meaning that supply and demand are always brought into balance. And when supply and demand are out of balance, forces emerge that either increase or decrease production or consumption, and supply and demand go back into balance. The process keeps our retail stores fully stocked; it keeps the infrastructure in the industrial system functioning, and it keeps goods and services moving in a balanced and appropriate way.

But that balance cannot exist in a centrally planned economy, except by accident. Unless the central planners—by some extraordinary luck—determine a bill of goods that should be produced that is identical to what all their consumers would want, they are going to make a mistake. Eventually, they will have a shortage of one good and a surplus of others. And, indeed, what we saw in the stores in the Soviet Union and Eastern Europe during the heyday of central planning was gluts of some goods, while other products were not available at any price. In other words, they could never get it right because there is no way to get it right when a group of planners tries to determine in advance what individuals will want. And those individual wants will occur in a market economy and in a centrally planned economy. You cannot make people buy things they do not want.

In a centrally planned economy, markets are cleared by a balance of ration coupons or queue or privilege, all of which proliferate. If a shortage of goods occurs, one way in which the "market" will work is essentially to force people to line up. If the line gets long enough, it will discourage enough people to bring demand down to the level of supply. Obviously, an extraordinary element of corruption is implicit in that type of system because privilege must and always does manifest itself, creating the availability of goods and subsidies to certain groups and not to others.

I describe this theoretical structure because it is important to understand how different what has evolved on the other side of the Iron Curtain for 40 years is from the structure we have in the West and why the transition is going to be so difficult. You have to restructure the basic systems, the mechanisms by which things are done. You have to set up financial instruments and financial structures. Commercial banks distinct from central banks must be developed. Securities markets must be set up; these are not play things or casinos that are irrelevant to the Western market economies. Securities markets are crucial elements that enable a society's value preferences to work their way through prices of goods, services and other claims to assets that, in turn, produce goods and services in a manner that optimizes the allocation of resources in the system. Setting up a stock exchange comes later in the process. What Eastern Europe needs first are financial markets.

More specifically, after Eastern European countries have completed the early stages of a financial system by separating the central bank function from the commercial bank function, they will need securities markets. *Securities markets* are the mechanisms by which the degree of liquidity in the system, meaning the degree of claims that one has on various goods and services, can be indicated in terms of time. In other words, a securities market enables you to have a claim that is payable in two days, six months, 10 years or 30 years.

We have such a mechanism in the West, and it endeavors to keep the integration, the interface, of our financial system with the physical production system going in a manner that optimizes competitive forces, and, therefore, economic growth and standards of living. Establishing something comparable in Eastern Europe is going to require considerable work. But it will be easy compared with the really deep-seated, fundamental problem that must be attacked if the transition from centrally planned to market economies is going to be pulled off. The major issue is essentially the philosophical value preferences of the society.

The Philosophical Transition from Central Planning to Market Economies

How individuals organize themselves in producing goods and services is a profoundly philosophical issue. It relates to concepts of right and wrong, what is valuable or not valuable, what is exploitation or not exploitation, what is fair trade, what is appropriate or inappropriate and, most fundamentally, what in the institutions is ethical or non-ethical. A society cannot be organized around a principle by which individuals deal with one another in a way they perceive, at root, to be unethical.

In all the educational systems that have evolved since the end of World War II on the other side of the Iron Curtain, the notions of markets, profit, competition and entrepreneurship are pejorative. Whereas, in many cases, we in the West perceive these concepts as notions of higher value and advancement of civilization, in the East these terms describe the way in which individuals should *not* deal with one another. And yet, unless those notions become pervasive and respectable in the East you cannot have a transition because the system will not allow it.

A major precondition to the East's transition to a market system will be its philosophical transformation. Essentially, this transformation requires changing the educational system structure. Recently, schools in East Germany basically taught one semester under a Marxist, centrally planned philosophy and all its accoutrements, then stopped, and started teaching a different regimen without any discussion of what the past was. As far as I know, it seems to have worked. But there has to be some kids saying, "But, Teacher, last term you told us exactly the opposite." How that will work, I do not know. But I do know that this issue will be the most profoundly difficult problem that confronts the way in which the system functions.

I am fond of using a joke I heard in Moscow in 1989. In a sense, the joke describes what is wrong. There are two different stores in Moscow. Both sell pineapples—one for five rubles a piece and the other for one ruble a piece. Everyone knows that the one-ruble-a-piece store does not have any pineapples. Nonetheless, the story goes, the queue to buy pineapples is at the store where the price is one ruble, and there is no queue at the five-ruble store. The reason, we are told, is that one ruble per pineapple is the right price. The five-ruble price is confiscatory, too speculative and profit-oriented, and we should not in any way partake of that.

In a sense, we are looking at the historic roots of the philosophy underlying centrally planned systems. The philosophy relates in part to the medieval concept of just price, to which, I might add, usury is also linked. So, we are dealing with profoundly important issues, not of economics, but of philosophy and value preference.

When one looks at the tug-of-war going on in the Soviet Union between the various economic plans, the problem is not that some protagonists of going slow in the Soviet Union think that central planning works. They do not. But they are acutely aware that the underlying view of markets and how one behaves within them has not changed in the Soviet Union. And they are acutely aware that this process must be changed. But how one reconciles the economic need for cold-turkey, quick shifts from central planning to markets and the very difficult issue of changing a society's underlying philosophy overnight, I cannot say. I do say that this is the crucial issue in understanding and projecting the success of the transition underway in the centrally planned economies of the East.

The outcome is profoundly important to all of us in the West. Change in Eastern Europe will be very difficult, but look at the alternative. A monumental event that occurred over a very few weeks in 1989 has moved the world back from nuclear confrontation, back from having two fundamentally different societal systems behaving in an increasingly antagonistic way. We have witnessed an extraordinary event that people 100 and 200 years from now will look back on as one of those crucial points in human history.

So far as civilization is concerned, so far as peace is concerned, we must be of assistance to this transition. The unraveling of this 40-year experiment in a relatively few days and weeks in 1989 is of extraordinary importance in the world. That is why, as I said in my opening remarks, it is terribly important to differentiate what is happening in Eastern Europe from the crucial events in the Middle East. The outcome in the Middle East will be important to our societies but relatively minor compared with the extraordinary events of 1989.

A Decade of Decisions

Admiral Bobby R. Inman, USN (retired)

It is a particular pleasure for me not only to see a lot of familiar faces but also to see most of the places filled. Four years ago, when under Bob Boykin's leadership the Dallas Fed began to step out more in sponsoring conferences to look at the economy in this region, there were some skeptics in Washington, D.C., who wondered whether this was a viable role—whether our role was not entirely simply to feed statistics to Washington, where someone would decide what they meant and what needed to be done.

I am persuaded that this series has already established a tradition of helping to create an environment in which we can look forward. What are the issues? Where can we all work together? The reality is that you people are the ones who will make the economic growth of the 1990s a reality.

As I look at this decade, there are more uncertainties than at any time in my adult life. There may be more opportunities, but we are dealing with a world that is changing at an incredible pace. Many things that were certainties all my adult life are now changing.

To have sustained economic growth, you must have broad political stability, readily available capital at affordable rates, a skilled and motivated work force and a strong base of science and technology, and you must capitalize on all those factors. There are many other features that the private sector alone can add and must add—a focus on quality, innovation, safety and environmental matters. All these will be important in the 1990s in the outcome of what this economy will look like. But it is the pace of change in the broadest sense in the outside world on which I want to focus for awhile.

After Communism: The Soviet Union and Eastern Europe in the 1990s

1989 catapulted us into this new decade. Those of us who spent our lives in the national security arena suddenly got all the things we had ever hoped for. But what we had not counted on was that the events would happen in such an incredibly short time frame, events such as the collapse of communism as a form of government. The failure of communism in the economic system had been apparent for some years, but it was not at all clear that it would translate into peaceful political change. Then suddenly on November 8, 1989, came the end of the Berlin Wall, which was preceded by Poland's accepting a non-communist government and the Hungarians' willingness to allow East Germans to flee across the Hungarian border to Austria. In less than a year, the landscape of Europe has changed. There is now one Germany.

In the Soviet Union, the jury is very much still out. Even as we are gathered here, Soviet President Mikhail Gorbachev is scrambling for what almost amounts to a vote of confidence before his own parliament on the issues of the collapsing economy and the political direction of the country. Fourteen of the 15 republics are asserting their right for independence and are running all their affairs. The great issue is, What is the stability of the military? Will the union hold together as Gorbachev continues to try to assert political authority?

The signs of how difficult this was going to be were paramount last spring when Gorbachev came to the United States. His accompanying entourage, most of whom had been with him the five-plus years he has been in power, were, in private, critical of Gorbachev's performance, his indecision and his difficulty making the hard decisions. They were worried about the frittering away of public support. It almost sounded like presidential assistants I have heard over the past six administrations criticizing the president for his performance, which is not heard of when dealing with Soviet leadership. Probably more important was the almost uniform view among those advisers that as much as Gorbachev detested Boris Yeltsin, he would have to deal with Yeltsin. Yeltsin had just been elected president of the Russian Republic while Gorbachev was on that trip. It was clear that Yeltsin, demagogue and heavy drinker that he is—neither of which distract from political support in the Soviet Union, had the popularity to make the hard choices that Gorbachev no longer had.

The best case for the Soviets is to hold together the union, let the Russian Republic take the lead in economic development and perhaps aim toward spinning off the Baltic republics and the troublesome provinces along the southern border into independent states, which will be economic basket cases. That is a Soviet Union, an evolving Russia, that still has an awesome supply of nuclear weapons as well as some potential economic strength if they can manage their economy. But it must be financed. Gorbachev's best hope for this optimistic scenario is to give back the Kuril Islands toward the end of the year or early next year before he goes to Tokyo in April and get the same kind of warm reception that he is accustomed to getting in Washington, not in Moscow. Then, with that money, he will have three years to try to turn around the economy. The odds are remote that he can be successful to the degree of being elected when he finally has to go to the public, but he has the prospect of at least passing authority to elected leadership that will be committed to a market economy.

The worst case is that the Soviets cannot control the conversion, that there are strikes followed by food riots followed by an order for the military to crack down, and the military comes apart when the political commissar is no longer there to assure control.

Chaos in the Soviet Union is not in the United States' long-term economic interest. I dwell on this for some length because how those events play out—and we have relatively little control over them—will have a lot to do with the phase of political stability in much of Europe.

In what we have called Eastern Europe, which we are now beginning to refer to as Middle Europe, the good news of the political conversion is behind us. The really tough days are ahead in trying to create market economies that work. The individuals who live in those states will be increasingly disillusioned as they face hard economic realities, and they do not see a prospect for an early turnaround.

Complicating that situation are enormous stresses on the fabric of society within those countries—rivalries among provinces. One of the leaders of the Polish revolution refers to it as looking more like Europe in 1910 than we had anticipated it would look in 1990. Separatist activities in Czechoslovakia, Hungary, Romania and Yugoslavia will add much complication to the effort to develop vibrant, market-driven economies.

Decisions Ahead for Europe, Asia, Latin America, Africa and the Middle East

I will skirt around most of the events in Western Europe, not wanting to trip over the remarks of our keynote speaker, but a political change is coming, with full activation of the Common Market in 1992—with already the certainty of a single monetary system but not yet the certainty of a single overseeing banking system—and still some momentum from at least Germany and France toward a political union as well. But there is substantial resistance to a union in some of the other countries. As we watch next week the struggle for leadership of the Conservative Party in Great Britain, we may well get some clear sign of whether political union will become the driving force or whether there will be a sustained resistance that will keep the Common Market purely at the level of the world's largest marketplace. But that in itself is a dramatic impact as we think about the world through the 1990s and on to the turn of the century.

In looking back at China at the mistake that many of us made when looking at events there while anticipating faster economic growth, there was a belief that the 80-year-olds really had turned over power. It was a great act when Deng

Xiaoping walked off stage and took all his fellow 80-year-olds with him. But in fact, they did not turn over control, and we learned that visibly at Tiananmen Square on June 4, 1989. We probably will have three or four years until ill health removes those 80-year-olds from the scene and another four or five years after that of a scramble for power before it is very clear who will run that great country in the 21st century. Until that is done, China remains one of the great question marks on the international stage.

Events in East Asia continue to move at a very rapid pace in economic activity, but political change is also hovering out there in the wings. A political change driven in large measure by a change in economic circumstances and the dramatic change of perceptions of the Soviet Union as a threat may well lead, before the 1990s are over, to an environment in which economic pressures drive events in Korea, and the U.S. military involvement there since 1950 will dwindle to a very small presence, if there is any at all. In the Philippines, we may see a decision in 1991 that lets the United States retain use of the Subic Bay naval installation but give up Clark Air Base, but the odds are very high that by 1996 we will be out of the Philippines entirely. Therefore, U.S. forces deployed in the Pacific, if there are any beyond Guam, will rest on Japanese soil. Of course, the critical issue in the United States' relationships with Japan will be how we manage the economic relationships in a very changed world. But I remind you that political change—generational political change—is likely to occur in Japan in this decade. It almost got accelerated in 1989 by the Recruit scandal. That situation was avoided, but now the most recent turmoil about whether to deploy Japanese military forces outside Japan to the Persian Gulf again came close to toppling the leadership from power, but they drew back and probably are successfully past this latest hurdle. But change will come. We do not know nearly enough about the next generation of political leaders. Only occasional glimpses tell us that they may be more nationalistic, more arrogant about their own economic strength and less inclined to make compromises based on national security concerns.

In Latin America, the growth of democracy has been very heartwarming in the late 1980s, but it has not yet been accompanied by the kind of economic promise that says there is new stability in that region, even less so as you move toward Central America.

In Africa, we have the first glimmers of what could be political success in transition away from apartheid and a very changed relationship in the southern cone of Africa for economic development. But change is coming along painfully slowly, and it rests on the continued health, well-being and governance of a small handful of people. Violence could disrupt it, and for much of the rest of Africa the news is as unhappy as in other parts of the world as one looks at the prospect of tribal divisions that threaten the economic structures of countries that were put in place back in the Colonial era.

Finally, in the Middle East, events will play out in the next six to eight months with regard to the Iraqi invasion of Kuwait. I do not know how the events will play out, but what is clear is that it will change how the Arab world has worked in the past, with all the impact you will hear discussed about oil. If we are lucky enough to get out without a very bloody conflict and without the continued overhanging threat of the use of weapons of mass destruction on other countries, then there will be a chance to re-assess the role of international organizations. Indeed, if we have a happy outcome, it will be largely the result of success in getting the United Nations to function in this instance as it was originally intended to function in 1945 but has never been able to do so because of a great power rivalry.

16-Million-Bit Chips, Biotech and Microstructures: Technological Turning Points in the 1990s

Even as we go through that swirl of political change and the economic change that is accompanying it, there is also an incredible quickening of pace in the world of science and technology. Las Vegas is now hosting a big trade show for the computer industry, and already some marvelous advances are being displayed. But these advances are barely curtain-risers for what this decade offers. Five years ago we thought it would be a great development to cram a million bits of information on a single chip. Now we have chips holding 4 million bits each, and 16-million-bit chips will be available in the fairly near future. As one looks at the incredible ability to compact information in smaller and smaller packages, the economic impact of change can barely be foreseen. Just to demonstrate for those of you who are not computer buffs, the first large-scale computer was built in 1944 to support the U.S. cryptologic attack on German and Japanese codes. That machine filled a space almost as large as this ballroom. By the middle 1980s, power a hundred times that of the 1944 machine was found in a small, portable personal computer that would sit on half this podium. Today, just five years later, more than 10 times that power is found in a single chip. That is the pace by which change is coming in the information-handling world.

In the world of biotechnology, changes are equally dramatic. Such changes include the understanding of the human genome; the ability to isolate a single cell and to begin to attack illnesses in a very different way; the prospect that one can deal with growth factors and childhood illnesses in ways that we had never dreamed possible even five years ago; the dramatic impact that one can see in therapeutic efforts to help the healing process, for all the impact that has on reducing permanent damage or death from injuries, accidents and of course the impact of significantly raising the prospect of survival for individuals in military conflicts. And many more dramatic changes are lurking.

In the materials area, it really is the decade of chemists and their ability to let us put together microstructures—an operating engine that is about the size of a human hair in its cross section. Early experimental work has already been undertaken at Cal Tech to offer the potential of surgical instruments implemented through the bloodstream well before the 21st century. The push from technology will continue to be very dramatic across a large number of areas.

Equally dramatic for those of us here in the Southwest is the reality of changes from demographics. If you look back at the birth rates of the 1980s for the country at large and then focus on this region, the birth rate for young Anglo women of child-bearing age remained fairly steady at 1.7 throughout the decade. For young black women of comparable age, the rate was 2.3 for the first half of the decade and 2.5 for the last half. For young Hispanic women in the same age bracket, the rate was 2.7 for the first part of the decade and 2.9 for the last half, heading toward 3. When you look even closer at the numbers, especially the ones for blacks, what is particularly striking and alarming is that the birth rate among young, married black women is almost exactly the same as their Anglo counterparts. So, the great spurt in the birth rate has been among unmarried blacks. This trend raises many issues for us in a skilled and motivated work force in the 1990s and beyond.

As one looks particularly at this region, the population shift is occurring so fast that probably before the turn of the decade, if we are able to hold even a reasonable portion of youngsters in school, more than half those leaving 12th grade to enter the work force will be non-Anglo—a very dramatic shift. If we are not successful in keeping kids in school, the consequences will be grim. You need only look at the latest statistics on school dropouts to understand the magnitude of the problem in front of us. Texas was running 48th in the country in the number of school dropouts; we now have reached the unenviable position of 50th among the 50 states. In the largest prison system in the country, nine out of 10 inmates are school dropouts.

As one contemplates the challenge of molding a skilled and motivated work force that ensures a vibrant, growing economy, we face a very major challenge indeed. I will leave to the speakers who come after me the challenge of giving you solutions to these problems.

PART TWO

The Changing International Marketplace

"History is accelerating to hyperspeed. What was unthinkable only yesterday is unremarkable now."

—Richard W. Fisher

"[T]he establishment of a national market between the two Germanys, from one day to the other, was the most severe shock therapy ever used in recent economic history."

—Christian Watrin

"The Mexican option to locate certain activities in Mexico may, in fact, be crucial to help some U.S. firms survive and provide high-quality jobs in the United States."

—James R. Markusen

America Has Made the World Safe for Democracy. Now What?

Richard W. Fisher

Ulysses S. Grant used to say that he knew only two tunes. One was *Yankee Doodle*, and the other wasn't. Since I returned from Japan in May, I have come to feel like I know only two things: one is Japan, and the other isn't.

What Was Unthinkable Is Now Unremarkable

I know you came to hear me speak about Japan. But it struck me as I thought about what I might say today that it is not just Japan's ascendancy that marks the end of an era. Three weeks ago, I had the pleasure of briefing President F.W. de Klerk of South Africa on the Democratic Party, which, incidentally, he concluded (correctly) was like trying to explain non-Euclidean geometry. In contemplating that experience and the initiative President de Klerk has taken to change the status quo in his country, it struck me that America's crusade for freedom and democracy, begun as an isolated, unprecedented experiment in governance some 214 years ago, has finally taken grip in the world at large. History is accelerating to hyperspeed. What was unthinkable only yesterday is unremarkable now.

- South Africa is dismantling apartheid.
- The Gorbachev devolution of the Soviet empire and the Yeltsin revolution in Russian governance is happening before our eyes.
- Czechoslovakia, Hungary, Poland and Romania have shaken off the shackles of communist repression and embarked on the road to market capitalism.
- The German Democratic Republic (GDR) has *voted* itself out of existence,

and Germany has been reunited under democratic rule.

- In our own hemisphere, dictatorial rule has fallen by the wayside in Chile, Panama and Nicaragua. Democracy is flourishing in Latin America.
- Mexico, once a thorn in our side, has declared openly and loudly its intention to join its future to that of North America, and we have endorsed that intention.
- Even Canada, which many of us had come to view as a vichyssoise of nations—cold, half French and difficult to stir—is undergoing a constitutional revolution.
- And, of course, Japan has notified us that it can, and very likely will someday, take Nancy Reagan's advice and "just say no" to American hegemony.

In light of this incredible panoply of developments, I thought it would be interesting today to broaden the subject somewhat and ask, Now what? Where do Americans go from here?

Germany and Japan help focus the mind.

In October 1990, the two German nations that emerged after World War II were united. The blitzkrieg of events that have led us to reunification has left most of our heads spinning. Many of us are unsure what all this means. Should we celebrate the affair, or should we fear it?

Let me suggest four points for you to consider, for they illustrate the broader points at hand. First, we must remember that reunification has all along been the goal of American foreign policy in Europe. And, without exception, the European governments are also in favor of a united Germany. Even in the U.S.S.R., with its dark memories of war with the Nazi German army, the leadership has given its blessing to unification, knowing full well that what most threatens Soviet security is internal economic and political chaos, not the threat of external might.

Second, it is important to remember that, as Chancellor Helmut Kohl recently said, "This is the first unification in modern history occurring without war and without suffering...." Not a single shot was fired to regain German soil from its repressive occupier.

I have had the privilege of knowing most of the major actors in this drama—Helmut Schmidt and Helmut Kohl as chancellors, Foreign Minister Hans Dietrich Genscher and most of the others who have made reunification possible. While they have carefully nurtured the growth of democracy within the Federal Republic of Germany for four decades, deep in their souls they have never been proud of the fact that democracy in West Germany, after all is said and done, was imposed from the outside by the occupying powers—France, England and the United States. Deep in their hearts, for 45 years they have been eager to show the world and prove to themselves that the German people are capable of achieving democracy on their own. To them, it is of overriding importance that it was an East German democratic revolution that overcame the Soviet occupier and not the massive military arsenal collected on West German soil. Those who worry about Germany reverting to its old ways should remember this. Their record of the past 45 years and their triumph of this past year provide compelling evidence of an abiding commitment to the democratic way.

Third, as we look to the Soviet Union, we must remember what made this recent experience with Germany so much more successful than that which followed their defeat in World War I. If there is a case in Europe for anyone to take on the characteristics of Germany in the 1930s, it is the Soviet Union today. We must handle diligently Soviet desires for security and prestige and prosperity. Otherwise, the nascent democracy beginning to raise its head in Moscow could give rise to extremism or anarchy or renewed authoritarianism, destabilizing the consolidation of democracy elsewhere.

A fourth point that needs to be mentioned is that a phenomenal amount of capital will be required to rebuild the GDR, Eastern Europe and what is now the Soviet Union, to say nothing of the capital that will be needed to exploit the opportunities presented by enhanced economic integration of Europe under the so-called *1992* initiative.

America is no longer the sole magnet for capital seeking a safe return. Gone are the days when we could confidently assume we could garner 70 percent of Japan's capital outflows or the savings of Middle Eastern potentates or the ill-gotten gains of Latin narcothugs. With the death of communism, capitalist yearnings are flourishing all over the world. We now have serious competition for the money we once took for granted. If one adds up the bill for German unification as I do—at close to $1 trillion in all—then add to it the cost of financing the reconstruction of the economies of Eastern Europe, the U.S.S.R., Mexico and Latin America *and* add to that the funds needed to privatize Britain's and Western Europe's state-owned assets *plus* the tab for recapitalizing the overleveraged private sector of the United States, the funds required to privatize the assets our banking regulators have nationalized *and* the cash flow needs of the U.S. government, the amount of capital needed in this world is truly staggering.

Japan: Check-Writer of the 1990s

This scenario provides a convenient introduction to Japan. Tokyo may not be Berlin, but—forgive me for saying so—it is still germane. Let me summarize Japan's position in the world by recalling a story once told by an aide to Willy Brandt, the former German chancellor and Nobel Prize winner. When Brandt was mayor of West Berlin, he visited Israel and was invited to view the great new Mann Auditorium in Tel Aviv. Having expressed his appreciation of Israel's naming the concert hall for Thomas Mann, the famous German writer, Brandt was promptly corrected by his host. The hall, he was told, was named for Frederic Mann of Philadelphia. "What?" bellowed Brandt. "What did he ever write?"

"A check," came the answer.

The blunt fact is that Japan has been the check-writer of the 1980s. As the largest repository of savings in the world, the Land of the Rising Sun has been the supplier of capital to those indisposed to saving on their own.

The charts and tables in Appendixes A and B define in great detail the sources and amounts of Japanese external capital flows. The following points deserve emphasis:

- From 1985 to 1989, Japan invested $181 billion net in U.S. securities. (To put this in perspective, Germany, whom many consider to be a great capital exporter, bought only $6 billion net over the same time frame.)
- Japan has purchased 10 percent of Canada's outstanding debt.
- Japan has become a crucial financier for Mexico and has quietly been providing aid to Panama, Nicaragua and other areas of strategic importance to the United States.
- Japan has channeled billions in investment, trade and aid into Southeast Asia, providing stability to a region rife with volatility.
- Japan has become the largest aid donor in Africa, surpassing France and England.
- Japan, of late, has been the major, if not sole, source of buying pressure in the German stock market and the French and European Currency bond markets.

Yet, a not unexpected thing has happened on the way to Japan's new-found economic and financial prominence. Japan has tired of adhering to the script whereby Washington proposes and Tokyo only disposes of money, a process increasingly derided in Tokyo as *nouveau riche* diplomacy.

It is better, as some say, to be *nouveau riche* than not *riche* at all. But at some point, a rich man wants to own his house, not rent it from others. At some point, a successful person wants to have a hand in writing the rules that govern his or her environment. After spending the first three months of 1990 in Japan and meeting with most of the country's leaders, I can tell you Japan is fast approaching this point.

Japan's Position in the Post–Cold War Era

America was shocked in 1989 with the appearance of the first translated copies of Shintaro Ishihara's *Japan That Can Say No.* Yet those who have been reading the Japanese daily press for the past decade were not surprised.

Japanese pride and self-assertiveness have been growing ever stronger in line with her economic success. Japan's bureaucratic mandarins have made it increasingly clear that they want to position their nation as an international force in the post–Cold War era. They want a seat at the United Nations Security Council. They talk of chairing the International Monetary Fund. They want to be accepted as full partners at summit meetings, such as the recent one in Houston, and at other gatherings of the great powers.

One senior Foreign Ministry official recently told me that "we are not willing to be the Saudi Arabians of the 1990s." I interpreted this statement as meaning that the Japanese are unwilling for long simply to rent our protection and remain themselves powerless. The Japanese want to have a hand in defining priorities, in initiating policy responses, in playing more than just a monied role in the implementation of solutions. (Let me add that if we show a failure of will in the Middle East, Japan will almost certainly accelerate its drive to become more independent.)

To be sure, some obstacles stand before Japan's accession to full partnership in the leadership of the world of the 1990s. Let me mention just two.

First, while Japan is a constitutional democracy, its form of government is distinctly different from all the rest. It is certainly different from ours. In the United States, everybody in government views himself or herself as a decisionmaker; in Japan, nobody makes decisions. And unlike the parliamentary democracies of England, Germany and France, the Japanese parliament has no real power, nor do the Japanese people. More than one observer of Japan has posited that if a Martian landed in Tokyo and said, "Take me to your leader," he would find that there is none. Japan is governed by an amorphous network of forces that the Dutch journalist Karel van Wolferen aptly describes as "The System."

The system, in van Wolferen's analysis, presents a variety of paradoxes. "It has no strong leadership, yet it creates the impression abroad of a purposeful giant bent on economic conquest of the world." It has no political center, yet it achieves consensus. It is ever-present yet elusive, not just to Westerners who want to deal with it but also to Japanese who participate in it. "It exists without most of its participants being consciously aware of it."

Because of its amorphous nature, the Japanese system will certainly be difficult to integrate into the club of great post–Cold War powers.

Second, Japan's financial structure is undergoing severe stress. The country's real estate market has reached levels of hyperinflation that threaten the banking system. And the recent plunge in the Tokyo stock market threatens to further cripple Japan's behemoth banks and securities houses. Whereas until now, Americans and Europeans were concerned that they might be overrun by

Japanese buyers, we might begin to see the Japanese unload not only U.S. Treasury bonds, but also the loans, buildings and companies they once bought so eagerly.

Growth in Japan's influence could be retarded if Japan closes its checkbook. This possibility and the inherent difficulty of dealing with the amorphous Japanese system will likely retard the eventual acceptance of Japan into the inner sanctum and its treatment as more of an equal.

America Reshapes the World in its Image

In short, history is witnessing the transformation of Germany and Japan. Whereas only yesterday the United States was, in effect, the sole proprietor of the enterprise of democracy and freedom, we now find ourselves presiding over a partnership. We have carefully nurtured the rebuilding of our former foes. They are now successful converts to the religion of market capitalism and are able to share the responsibility and the burdens of protecting and projecting freedom and prosperity throughout the world.

What does this mean for the United States, other than gratification for a job well done? Where is history taking us? The British scholar Arnold Toynbee once wrote that history was "something that happened to other people." Recently, *The Economist* noted that "these days Americans feel the reverse—that history is descending on them with a vengeance, pushing them out of the way. Having won the victory of this century with the collapse of the Soviet Empire, the citizens of the United States fear that they may be on the way to the dustbin, while Sony (of Japan) and Seimens (of Germany) stand poised to inherit the earth."

Many people here at home perpetuate this myth. We are bombarded almost daily with woeful tomes, such as Paul Kennedy's *Rise and Fall of Great Nations*, and shameful newspaper ads by Boone Pickens, declaring that we "lost the war to Japan" and pitiful requests by Dallas City Council member Al Lipscomb that recent immigrants and foreign investors go home "because we were here first and deserve the spoils."

Winston Churchill wrote that "history with its flickering lamp stumbles along the trail of the past, trying to reconstruct its scenes, to revive its echoes, and rekindle with pale gleams the passion of former days." Then he went on to ask, "and what is the worth of all this?" We cannot go back in time. Our passion must be directed to the future. I am amused that people now commonly assume that the U.S.S.R. will change, that Europe will change, that Japan will change, that Latin America will change, but that America is now static, as if the times have somehow dried up our nation, frozen it, cracked it and powdered it into dust. It just is not so.

Never forget the historical novelty that America represents. The American experience was the very first historical attempt to give back to citizens what the state had stolen from them. We were established as a radical experiment, and we conducted that experiment without entanglement for more than a century. Beginning with World War I, we were called on by our wealth and our zeal to project our experience to a larger world. For most of this century, we thus have been a crusader for freedom and democracy, defeating first the German imperialists, then the fascists and militarists of the 1940s and finally the communists. It is safe to say that we are winning our crusade. We are reshaping more than half the globe in our image.

Now, we must become the exemplar of liberty—we must show the world how democracy and capitalism can really work in the modern age. For this we are well equipped. As my friend and tutor, Joe Nye, has argued so eloquently, alone among the great nations, the United States possesses all the attributes of strength and permanence. We have abundant natural resources. We have a huge and flexible economy. We have a strong military that respects civilian authority. We have great universities and research centers. We are masters of high technology. We have an entrepreneurial culture. We share a universalist ideology. And we are possessed of a dynamic and ever-changing demography.

America: Asylum for Mankind

An ever-changing demography may be our greatest strength. Unlike any other country, if you are not happy where you are in the United States, you move to a place where you wish to be. Dallas provides ample testimony to this fact. This mobility does not happen in Japan or in Germany or in the United Kingdom. More important still, if you are hungry and eager to improve your lot, you come to the United States.

Thomas Paine spoke of America as "an asylum for mankind" almost 200 years ago. Two hundred years later, we remain as such. Almost 9 million immigrants entered the United States during the 1980s, accounting for 40 percent of the nation's overall population growth this past decade. To turn a phrase, immigration is the sincerest form of flattery.

Too often I hear the comment, "Yeah, but these are the wrong kinds of immigrants." Well, the complexion of our immigrants has indeed changed. Over the past decade, more than 80 percent of U.S. immigrants have been Hispanic and Asian, split 50–50. Only 13 percent have been Europeans. As the child of European immigrants, I note this statistic somewhat nostalgically but also in awe of the adaptability of our unique brand of democracy. Nowhere is it written that we must be an Anglo–European nation. Nowhere is it written that to succeed in this great country you must look like you and me. All that is assumed is that we are a free nation of equal opportunity.

The task we face as a nation is an awesome one: we are seeking to become the first great multiracial democracy in the history of mankind. This feat is not easy. Not a day passes when this phenomenon does not give rise to fear and friction, from the misguided musings of Dallas County Commissioner John Wiley Price to the prejudicial platforms of David Duke of Baton Rouge. Yet you and I know that this society will not be built by the racists or talkers, the self-promoters or the pretenders. It will be built by the doers.

Let me suggest that we are further along the curve than most people realize. What other country today or what other superpower in the history of the world can claim a society in which the highest office in the land is held by a white, the commander of its military is black, the chief executive officer of one of its most effective hallmark businesses (Coca-Cola) is Hispanic and 25 percent of the graduates of its finest universities are of Asian ancestry? These are the Americans of the new century. This is the America that is the exemplar of democracy. This is the America that will remain, when all is said and done, the world's greatest nation.

If you are ever tempted in a moment of doubt to concur with the naysayers and the doomsdayers, remember what Mark Twain said of the music of Wagner: "It is just not as bad as it sounds." The United States, to quote Nathan Glazer, is "a permanently unfinished country." Our society is unfinished. Our economy is unfinished. Our role in the world is unfinished. The American experiment never ends.

Appendix A
The Outlook for Japanese Money Flows

Chart 1
Japanese Current and Long-Term Capital Accounts

(Billions of U.S. dollars)

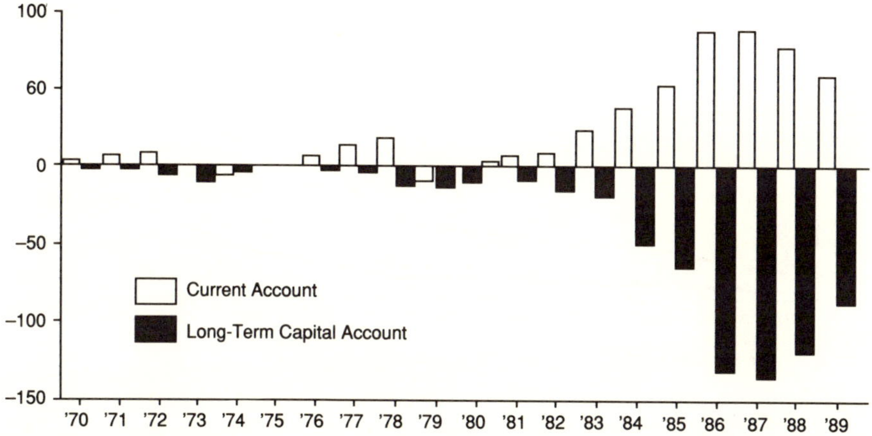

Source: Nomura Securities, Ltd.

Chart 2
External Position of Japan—Assets

(Billions of U.S. dollars)

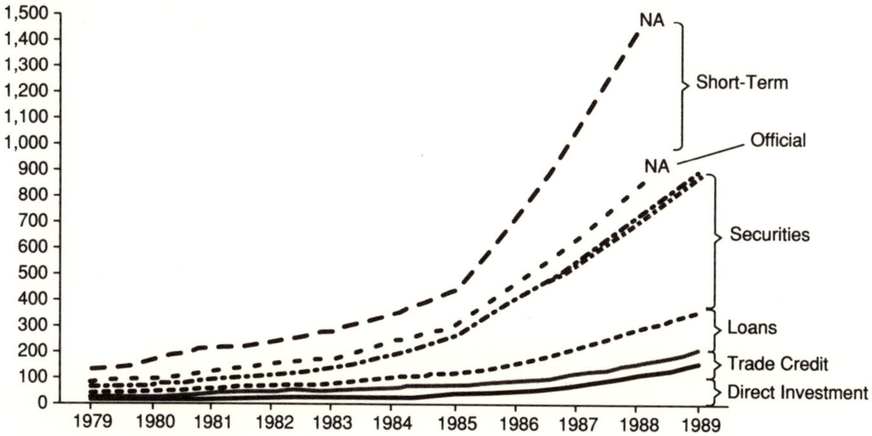

Source: Nomura Securities, Ltd.

Chart 3
External Position of Japan—Liabilities

(Billions of U.S. dollars)

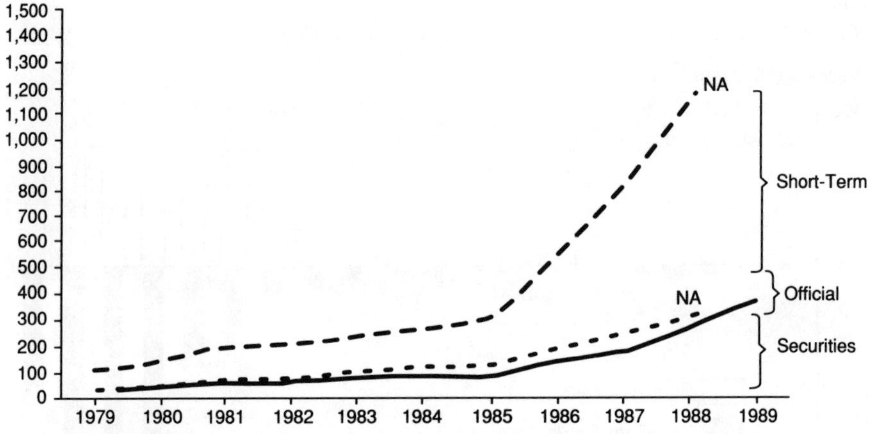

Source: Nomura Securities, Ltd.

Chart 4
Japanese Purchases Abroad

(Billions of U.S. dollars)

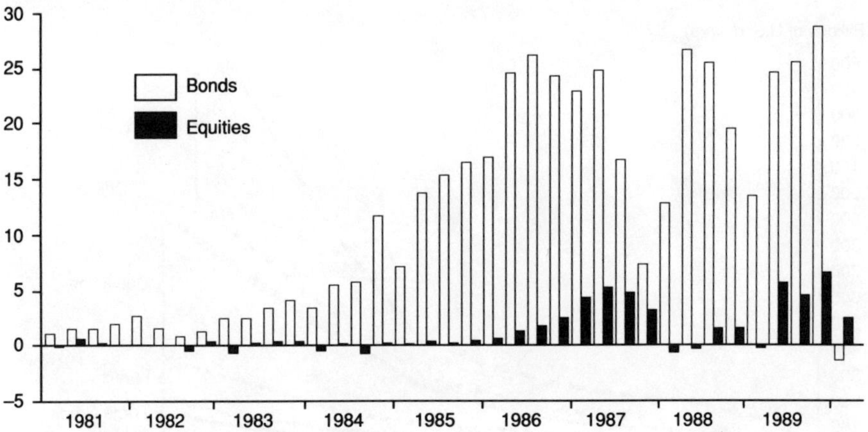

Note: 1990:1 figures are for January only.
Source: MOF

Chart 5
Foreign Purchases in Japan

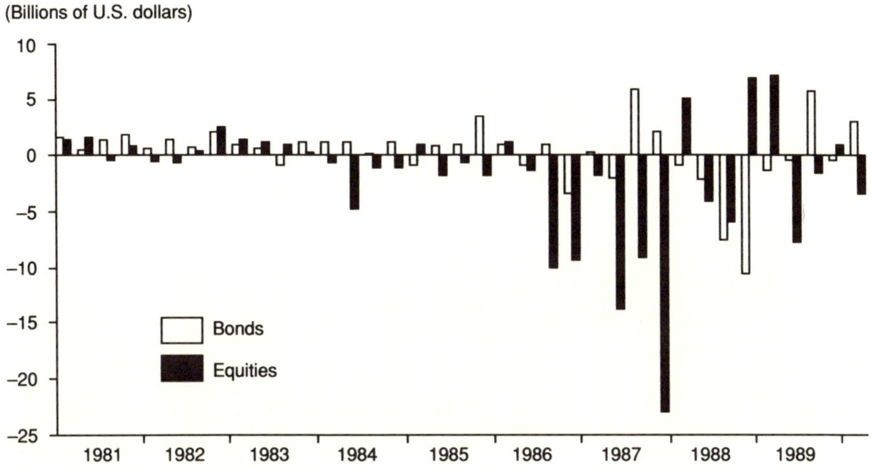

Note: 1990:1 figures are for January only.
Source: MOF

Chart 6
German Purchases of U.S. Securities

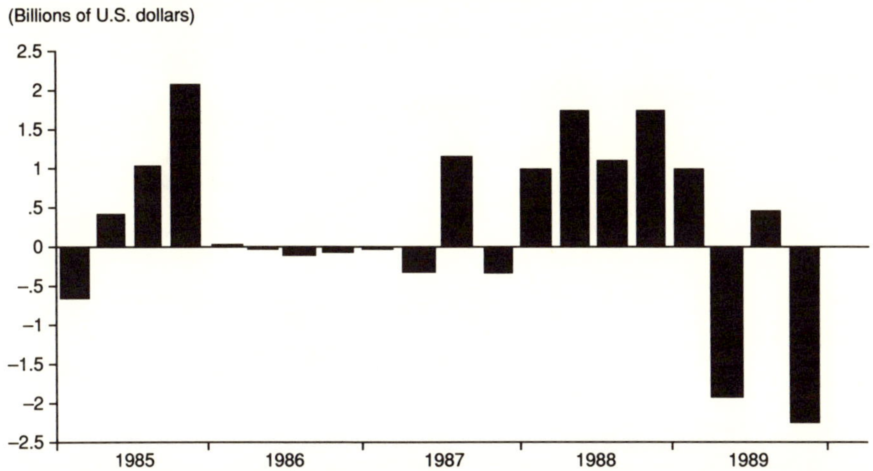

Notes: Figures are net purchases; Bonds and equities.
Source: Bundesbank

Chart 7
Japanese Purchases of U.S. Securities

(Billions of U.S. dollars)

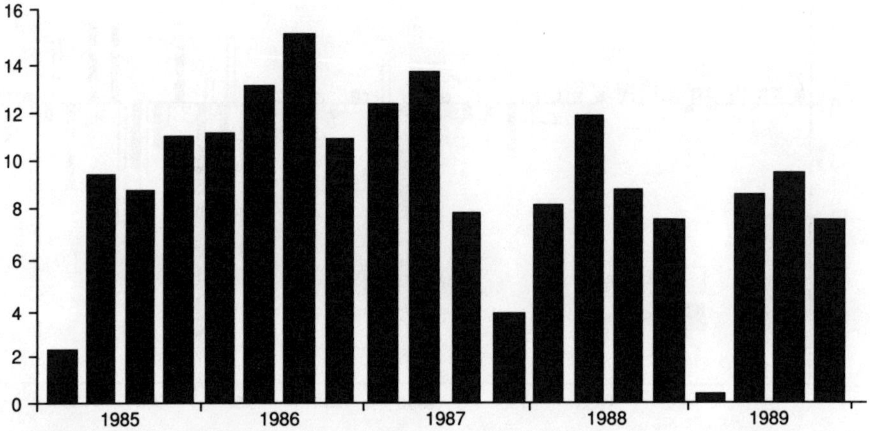

Notes: Figures are net purchases; Bonds and equities.
Source: MOF

Chart 8
Acquisition of Foreign Securities by Type of Investor

(Billions of U.S. dollars)

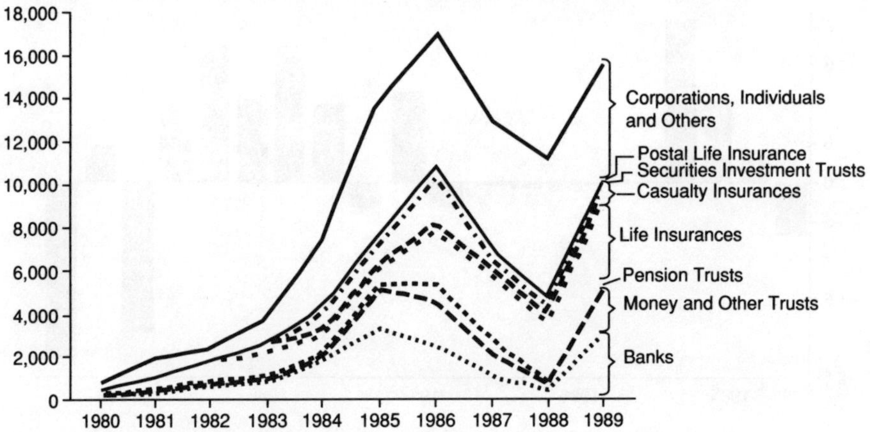

Source: Nomura Securities, Ltd.

Chart 9
Deregulation of Foreign Securities Investment

(Billions of U.S. dollars)

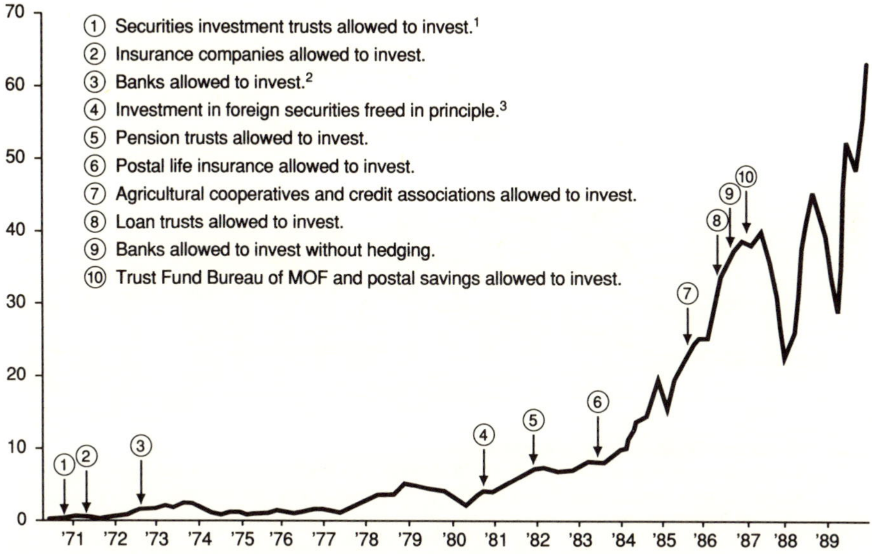

Notes: 1. Subject to prior approval by the MOF.
2. Subject to foreign exchange exposure limit.
3. Includes individuals and non-financial corporations.

Source: Nomura Securities, Ltd.

Chart 10
Foreign Investment by Life Insurance Companies

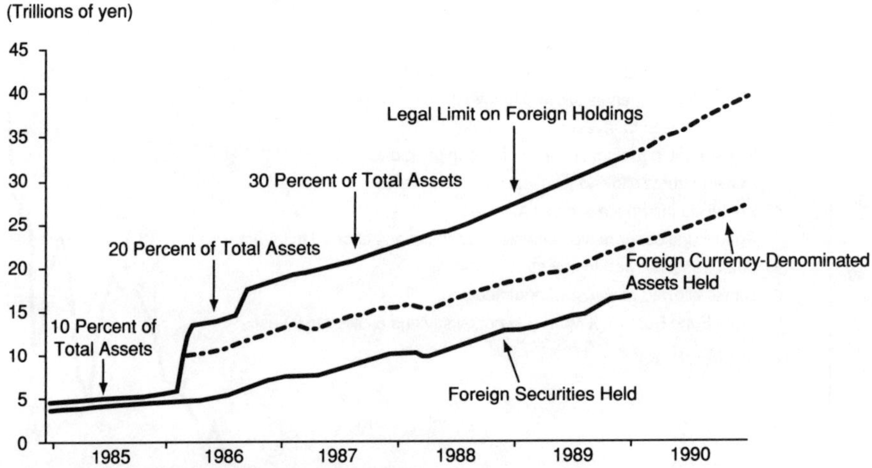

Notes: Figures after December 1989 are projections.
Foreign currency-denominated assets include foreign currency bank deposits and Sushi bonds (foreign currency-denominated bonds issued by Japanese corporations abroad).
Source: Nomura Securities, Ltd.

Chart 11
Foreign Securities Investments by Postal Life Insurance

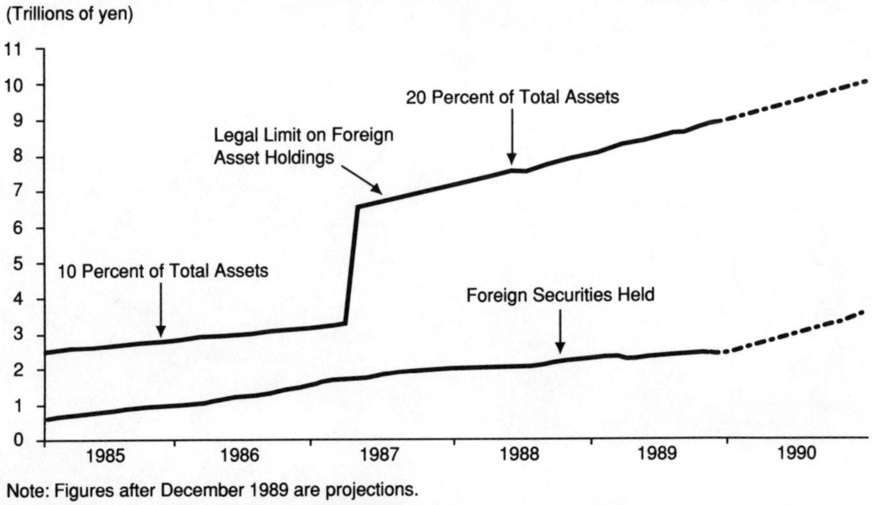

Note: Figures after December 1989 are projections.
Source: *Nihon Keizai Shinbun*, January 26, 1988.

Chart 12
Foreign Securities Held by Postal Life Insurance

(Trillions of yen)

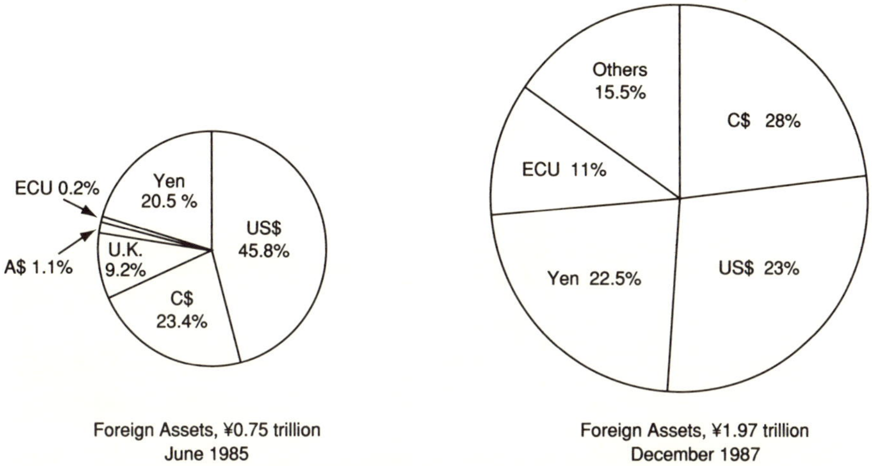

Source: *Nihon Keizai Shinbun*, January 26, 1988.

Chart 13
Foreign Asset Holdings of Securities Investment Trusts

(Trillions of yen)

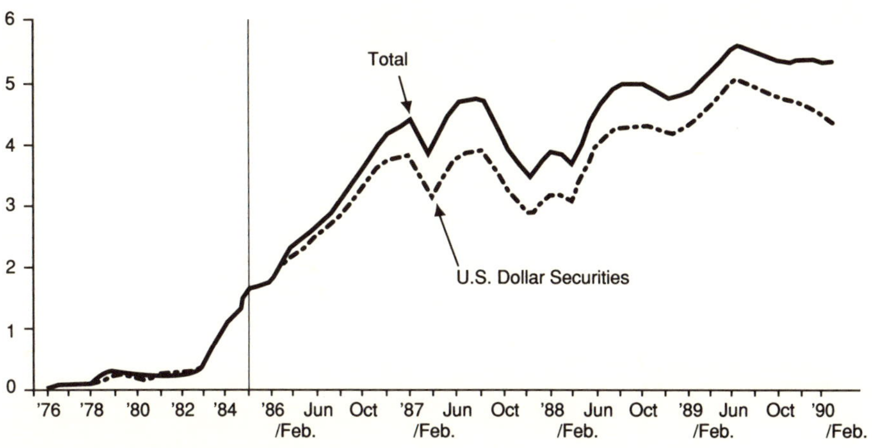

Source: Monthly Reports of Investment Trusts.

Chart 14
Foreign Securities Held by Securities Investment Trusts

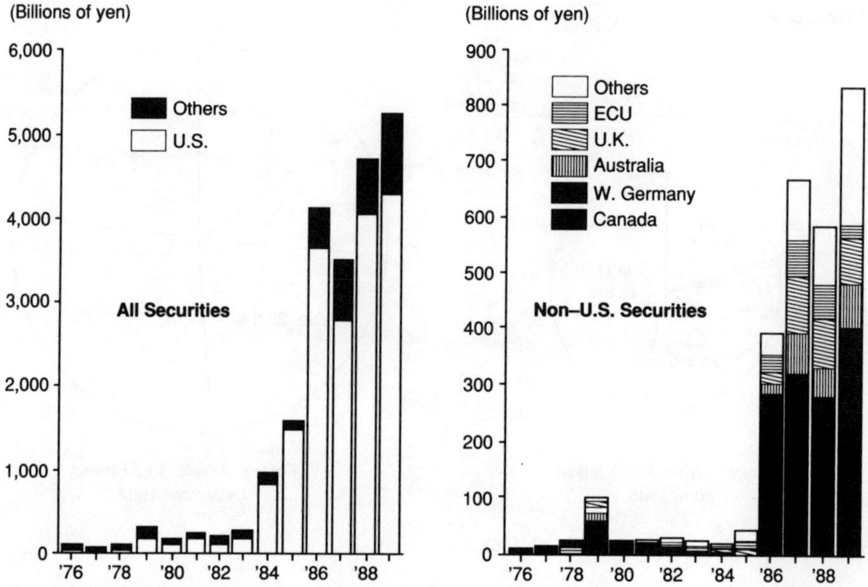

Source: Monthly Reports of Investment Trusts.

Chart 15
U.S. Trade Deficit and New Funds Available to Japanese Institutional Investors

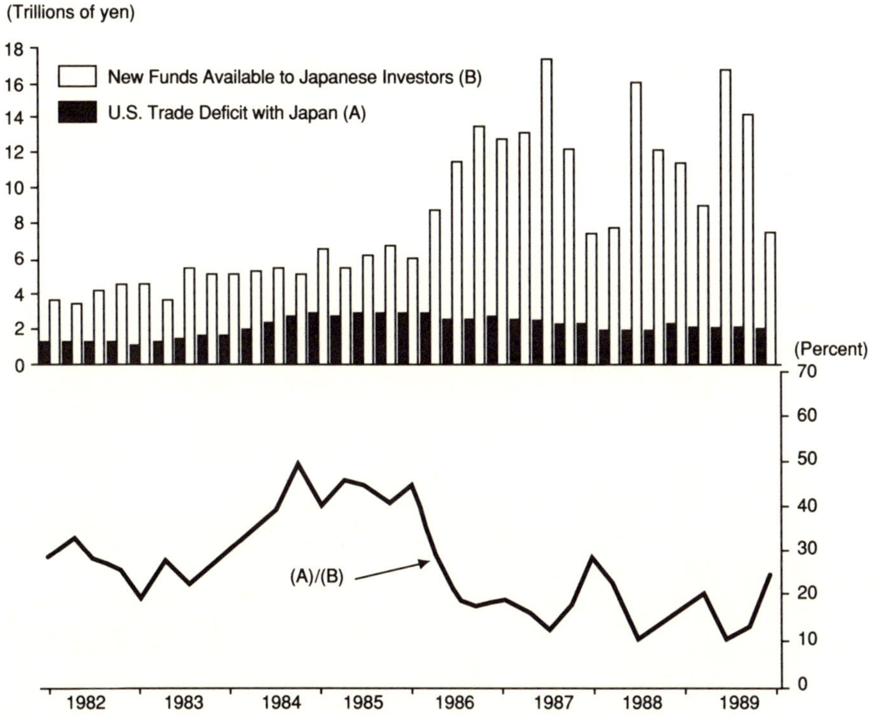

Note: Includes life and casualty insurances, postal life insurance, pension, loan and securities investment trusts.
Source: U.S. Department of Commerce, Bank of Japan.

Table 1
Net Purchases of Foreign Securities by Country

(Millions of U.S. dollars)

	Total	U.S.	U.K.	West Germany	Nether-lands	France	Luxem-bourg	Switzer-land	Australia	Canada	Others
4/77–3/78	942	581	195	26	6	–2	116	–1	0	6	15
4/78–3/79	9,728	8,416	809	92	52	15	210	–1	12	48	76
4/79–3/80	11,684	8,676	1,386	218	–34	–6	191	3	58	1,215	–23
4/80–3/81	19,672	13,371	1,375	229	91	46	844	36	65	3,465	132
4/81–3/82	7,856	2,056	1,816	451	107	–41	2,263	16	201	886	102
4/82–3/83	5,772	359	1,837	–100	–98	144	1,298	44	1,826	43	419
4/83–3/84	14,492	5,608	2,424	169	34	22	3,378	358	931	1,173	395
4/84–3/85	30,611	12,618	4,127	7	39	33	7,842	903	1,891	2,279	873
4/85–3/86	66,237	40,142	5,494	801	–16	39	13,492	353	296	1,818	2,818
4/86–3/87	111,188	50,718	14,521	4,321	93	726	27,158	263	86	5,518	4,786
4/87–3/88	74,908	33,296	6,717	4,931	646	800	22,037	303	2,060	165	3,951
4/88–3/89	90,199	28,373	10,881	5,574	653	816	33,782	891	588	3,775	4,870
CY 1985	55,406	31,271	6,192	433	–50	38	11,666	529	962	2,247	1,645
1986 Jan.	6,018	4,260	514	68	–3	–2	979	–22	–13	77	158
Feb.	6,225	3,648	781	246	9	7	1,393	–9	43	72	34
Mar.	5,916	3,236	–20	102	24	14	1,885	–5	–15	47	648
Apr.	11,673	6,736	1,619	204	20	58	2,085	11	194	262	485
May	9,051	3,916	1,355	178	27	41	2,576	5	14	321	619
June	5,840	2,281	1,506	87	2	42	1,408	3	128	317	66
July	9,345	4,619	1,192	320	–2	15	2,801	11	–172	356	205
Aug.	8,207	3,118	1,520	255	–34	50	2,466	8	–54	584	294
Sept.	11,038	7,107	707	327	13	54	1,790	8	–70	1,007	93
Oct.	8,434	3,271	895	276	–1	38	2,644	39	–28	1,012	289
Nov.	8,603	3,986	964	365	10	71	1,544	17	–138	1,308	477
Dec.	10,677	3,409	1,756	775	13	35	2,738	29	–185	1,279	828
CY 1986	101,027	49,587	12,789	3,203	78	423	24,309	95	–296	6,642	4,196
1987 Jan.	10,800	4,581	1,251	407	–6	14	3,136	18	–4	1,010	393
Feb.	11,184	6,727	694	484	37	52	1,821	60	146	729	435
Mar.	6,334	967	1,062	643	14	256	2,148	54	254	333	601
Apr.	9,473	2,085	933	2,237	73	401	2,819	29	462	71	362
May	7,440	3,308	787	105	241	71	2,018	56	185	44	625

June	13,934	8,169	1,033	1,180	118	31	3,095	17	160	–242	375
July	10,401	4,092	1,328	581	40	72	3,195	22	288	–35	819
Aug.	6,667	2,828	235	–115	24	35	2,637	16	266	–46	788
Sept.	3,543	838	466	225	–1	38	1,980	16	14	348	–382
Oct.	5,157	–39	464	–183	136	55	3,299	3	157	253	1,011
Nov.	3,716	3,471	–120	–110	–35	23	–66	15	369	254	–83
Dec.	1,963	365	546	183	–103	0	1,106	78	115	–216	–111
CY 1987	90,610	37,392	8,678	5,635	537	1,048	27,187	383	2,413	2,503	4,834
1988 Jan.	1,505	1,008	528	229	–6	10	18	20	80	–136	–247
Feb.	10,784	7,074	212	391	24	–10	2,760	33	0	1	300
Mar.	317	95	304	209	135	73	–824	–2	–36	–132	493
Apr.	7,400	2,549	651	1,175	32	75	2,431	22	248	183	33
May	11,684	6,892	735	840	112	129	1,785	61	102	734	295
June	7,713	2,359	1,055	854	113	125	2,351	43	–187	362	639
July	14,964	5,558	2,808	429	64	108	4,212	311	295	198	980
Aug.	8,946	4,239	915	–17	51	357	2,430	78	409	–218	703
Sept.	3,669	–990	737	229	10	–276	2,869	55	541	163	331
Oct.	7,524	2,460	555	461	100	5	2,390	92	274	249	939
Nov.	7,649	3,757	850	351	50	–38	2,198	44	–166	81	523
Dec.	6,752	1,213	1,350	883	75	5	2,828	147	246	–121	128
CY 1988	88,908	36,215	10,699	6,035	758	561	25,449	902	1,806	1,364	5,117
1989 Jan.	4,521	621	1,251	416	20	13	347	86	1,053	271	443
Feb.	11,883	5,473	–210	340	49	308	5,905	48	–726	165	531
Mar.	–2,506	–5,758	184	–387	–23	5	4,036	–96	–1,501	1,708	–675
Apr.	13,095	5,220	1,855	19	–167	180	6,651	66	–576	–1,868	1,714
May	8,378	2,412	1,382	435	101	208	1,036	0	2,085	–22	740
June	9,926	1,153	826	39	–39	465	5,612	136	1,084	–385	1,036
July	10,140	1,466	–197	622	219	613	4,836	120	988	731	742
Aug.	11,159	5,548	1,908	470	319	911	1,769	156	–1,790	509	1,358
Sept.	9,522	2,681	1,081	–30	–158	294	4,754	169	–250	787	194
Oct.	17,163	7,560	374	721	–136	747	4,724	133	524	1,003	1,511
Nov.	11,566	2,214	1,345	310	99	119	3,997	277	181	1,099	1,925
Dec.	8,824	–2,084	1,344	1,576	–32	–6	4,412	151	467	762	2,233
CY 1989	113,670	26,508	11,143	4,531	254	3,858	48,078	1,248	1,538	4,760	11,753
4/77–12/89	543,061	230,386	61,500	20,881	1,781	6,124	150,401	4,378	10,726	23,007	29,868

Notes: 1. Excludes Samurai bonds and short-term government papers.
2. Includes foreign currency-denominated bonds issued in Japan.
Source: MOF

Table 2

Discrepancies Between U.S., Japanese and German Data on Purchases of U.S. Securities

(Millions of U.S. dollars)

	German Purchases		Japanese Purchases	
	U.S. Treasury	Bundesbank	U.S. Treasury	MOF
1985:1	–2,707	–667	1,562	2,272
:2	3,120	432	6,664	9,250
:3	3,711	1,032	7,137	8,726
:4	2,163	2,029	7,020	11,023
Total	6,287	2,826	22,383	31,271
1986:1	1,752	31	4,411	11,144
:2	248	–34	7,347	12,933
:3	2,244	–125	14,722	14,844
:4	2,820	–112	355	10,666
Total	7,064	–240	26,835	49,587
1987:1	3,194	–90	7,350	12,275
:2	3,955	–288	9,639	13,562
:3	2,400	1,129	2,443	7,758
:4	2,901	–317	517	3,797
Total	12,450	434	19,949	37,392
1988:1	5,676	1,028	14,511	8,177
:2	–2,130	1,687	9,385	11,800
:3	–6,561	1,086	5,754	8,807
:4	–997	1,624	7,536	7,430
Total	–4,012	5,425	37,186	36,214
1989:1	811	936	6,603	336
:2	–2,432	–2,005	–5,645	8,785
:3	5,027	478	–142	9,695
:4		–2,226		7,690
Total		–2,817		26,506

Sources: MOF, Bundesbank

Table 3
Japanese Investment in U.S. Real Estate

(Millions of U.S. dollars)

By Location

State	Total through 1988	Percentage of total
Arizona	$1,730	4.03
California	$12,641	29.48
Florida	$683	1.59
Georgia	$848	1.98
Hawaii	$9,065	21.14
Illinois	$2,951	6.88
Massachusetts	$845	1.97
New York	$8,633	20.13
Texas	$1,720	4.01
Washington	$1,072	2.50
Others, plus D.C.	$2,696	6.29
TOTAL	$42,884	100.00

By Type*

Type	Total dollar amount	Percentage of total
Office	$8,310	50
Hotel/Resort	$3,577	22
Mixed-use	$2,416	15
Residential	$702	4
Retail	$644	4
Industrial	$310	2
Land	$302	2
Golf course	$202	1
Other	$81	less than 1
TOTAL	$16,544	100

*Purchased during 1988
Source: Kenneth Leventhal & Co.

Table 4
Japan's Three Major Investor Groups

I. Institutional Investors
   The two biggest investors are
   - Life insurance companies (long term) (¥110 trillion)
   - Securities investment trusts (short term) (¥57 trillion)

II. Non-financial Entities
   - Individuals (long term)
   - Corporations with large foreign currency cash flows (short term)

III. Banks
   - Must hedge all F/X exposure

Table 5
Composition of Foreign Currency-Denominated Securities Held by Life Insurance Companies

(Percent)

	September 1987	September 1988	September 1989
U.S. $	59	55	57
C $	19	16	15
A $	6	8	8
£	5	10	9
DM	2	4	4
FFr	1	2	3
ECU	4	3	2
Others	4	2	2

Source: Nomura Securities, Ltd.

Appendix B

Japanese Regulation and Guidelines on Investment in Foreign Assets

(as of March 20, 1990)

		Assets
LIFE INSURANCES	Foreign Securities:	30 percent of total assets. This limit includes yen-denominated foreign securities.
	Foreign CP, CDs:	3 percent of total assets.
	Loans to Foreigners:	10 percent of total assets. Only yen-denominated loans are permitted except in the case of investment in foreign real estate (see below). Exposure to a single borrower may not exceed ¥5 billion when extending the loan alone. In a syndicated loan, the share of insurance companies as a group may not exceed 50 percent of the total amount of the loan. (This 50-percent limit does not apply if the maturity of the loan exceeds 20 years.)
	Foreign Real Estate:	Must take the form of an investment in the local subsidiary that owns the real estate. The parent may purchase the stock of, or extend loans to, the foreign subsidiary. Such stocks are counted toward the 30-percent limit on securities, while such loans are counted toward the 10-percent limit on loans.
	Foreign Currency-Denominated Assets:	30 percent of total assets. This requirement applies to all foreign currency-denominated assets in the above four categories plus foreign currency-denominated bank deposits and foreign currency-denominated securities issued by Japanese corporations (for example, Sushi bonds). This requirement also applies to net outstanding buy contracts in foreign futures markets, such as U.S. Treasury bond futures. This requirement does not apply to those foreign currency-denominated assets that are hedged (such assets may still be subject to one of the four limitations above).

Foreign Bond, Interest Rate and Stock Index Futures and Options:	May be used for the purpose of hedging only. For those foreign contracts that relate to Japanese domestic bond instruments, the total (the sum of buy and sell) contracts outstanding may not exceed 50 percent of total domestic bond holdings. For those that relate to Japanese domestic equity instruments, total contracts outstanding may not exceed 50 percent of the current market value of domestic stock holdings. All other contracts outstanding, such as U.S. Treasury bond futures, may not exceed 50 percent of the comparable holdings of foreign currency-denominated assets. All buy contracts are counted toward the limits on holdings of various types of assets by life insurance companies.

In addition, foreign securities may be included in Special Money Trusts (Tokkins) held by these institutions, provided that the total amount of Tokkin accounts does not exceed 5 percent of total assets.

Valuation

Non-listed Securities:	These securities must be revalued if the exchange rate moves more than 15 percent against the book value of the investment. This rule is activated if the average exchange rate for March was 15-percent lower than the rate used last to calculate the book value of the investment. To calculate losses, the lower (weaker yen) of the average rate for March or the closing rate on the last business day of March is used. Only exchange rate changes, not price changes, are considered in the revaluation.
Foreign Currency Bank Deposits:	Same as non-listed securities.
Listed Securities:	Current price times the exchange rate prevailing on the last business day of the fiscal year.

For all assets, revaluation is allowed only in a downward direction. Exchange rate and price gains are not grounds for revaluation.

		Assets
CASUALTY INSURANCES	Foreign Securities:	30 percent of total assets. This limit includes yen-denominated foreign securities.
	Foreign CP, CDs:	3 percent of total assets.
	Foreign Loans:	10 percent of total assets. Only yen-denominated loans allowed. Exposure to a single borrower may not exceed ¥5 billion when extending the loan alone. In syndicated loans, the share of insurance companies as a group may not exceed 50 percent of the total amount of the loan. (This 50-percent limit does not apply if the maturity of the loan exceeds 20 years.) Borrowers are restricted to (1) foreign public-sector entities, including international organizations. (2) foreign banks with branches in Japan. (3) foreign private corporations that meet the requirements for issuing Samurai bonds. (4) those guaranteed by one of the above. (5) those with close shareholding ties with (3) above.
	Foreign Real Estate:	The combined total of domestic and foreign real estate holdings may not exceed 20 percent of total assets.
	Foreign Currency-Denominated Assets:	30 percent of total assets. This requirement applies to all foreign currency-denominated assets in the above four categories plus foreign currency-denominated bank deposits and foreign currency-denominated securities issued by Japanese corporations (for example, Sushi bonds). This requirement also applies to net outstanding buy contracts in foreign futures markets, such as U.S. Treasury bond futures. This requirement does not apply to those foreign currency-denominated assets that are hedged (such assets may still be subject to one of the four limitations above).
	Foreign Bond, Interest Rate and Stock Index Futures and Options:	May be used for the purpose of hedging only. For those foreign contracts that relate to Japanese domestic bond instruments, sell

	contracts outstanding may not exceed 30 percent of total domestic bond holdings. All other foreign sell contracts outstanding on interest rate futures may not exceed 30 percent of the sum of foreign currency-denominated bond and bank deposit holdings. For those foreign contracts that relate to Japanese domestic equity instruments, sell contracts outstanding may not exceed 30 percent of the current market value of total domestic stock holdings. All other foreign sell contracts outstanding on equities futures may not exceed 30 percent of total foreign equity holdings. Total outstanding sell contracts of foreign currency futures may not exceed 30 percent of foreign currency-denominated assets. All buy contracts are expected to result in deliveries and are counted toward the limits on holdings of those assets.
Gold:	3 percent of total assets.

Valuation

Basically the same as life insurance companies except for the use of the exchange rate on the last business day of March instead of the average for March and the treatment of non-listed securities. If the exchange rate moved more than 15 percent by the last day of March against the exchange rate used last to calculate the book value of non-listed securities, these companies must revalue these assets using the exchange rate and reasonable price quotations available from securities houses on March 31.

Assets

POSTAL LIFE INSURANCE, MINISTRY OF POSTS AND TELECOMMUNICATIONS	Foreign Securities: 20 percent of total assets. This limit includes yen-denominated foreign issues, such as Samurai bonds. No additional restrictions on bonds issued by foreign public-sector entities including international organizations and those guaranteed by such institutions. Corporate bonds must be publicly placed and issued by a listed company with capitalization of more than ¥6 billion. No equities permitted. Prefer bonds from those countries listed in the top

	20 of the country risk rating published by *Institutional Investor*. Must purchase securities via domestic offices of domestic and foreign securities houses.
	Valuation
	No requirement to revalue. Current yen values calculated at the end of each fiscal year only as references.
	Assets
POSTAL SAVINGS, MINISTRY OF POSTS AND TELECOMMUNICATIONS	Basically the same as the Postal Life Insurance. Limits on foreign asset holdings have not been established. Total funds available for investment in both domestic and foreign assets for fiscal 1987 were ¥2 trillion.
	Assets
TRUST BANKS	
Pension Trusts	Foreign currency-denominated assets: 30 percent of total assets. This includes bonds, equities, warrants, participation in investment trusts, CP, repos and real estate. The difference between the outstanding buy and sell contracts in foreign currency-denominated futures must remain within 50 percent of the amount of foreign currency-denominated assets held.
	Valuation
	For both independent and commingled funds, foreign securities are valued at the acquisition cost with current cash values calculated every day as references. For commingled funds, the return is calculated on the last business day of February and August, while for independently managed funds, which may have investments in commingled funds, the return is calculated on the last business day of March and September.
	Assets
Loan Trusts	Foreign bond holdings may not exceed 5 percent of total assets. Bonds only, no equities allowed. In principle, any foreign exchange risk must be hedged. Foreign futures may be used for hedging purposes only. The difference between the outstanding buy and sell contracts in foreign interest futures must remain within 50 percent of the holdings of comparable foreign bonds.

	Valuation
	Valued at the acquisition cost.
	Assets
Money Trusts	No limit on Special Money Trusts (Tokkins). For others, foreign bond holdings may not exceed 5 percent of total assets. Bonds only, no equities allowed.
	Valuation
	The valuation must be consistent with the accounting principle followed by the owner of the account (that is, insurance companies must use the lower of the acquisition cost or the market value method, while non-financial corporations may use the acquisition cost method).
	Assets
Securities Investment Trusts	Individually set up and approved by the Ministry of Finance. Foreign assets are generally limited to 50 percent of total assets, but many specialized funds have no limit. Listed stocks and bonds only. No foreign real estate, CP or CDs permitted. Buy contracts outstanding in foreign interest futures may not exceed the amount of expected cash flow that results from interest payments and the maturing of securities. Sell contracts outstanding may not exceed the face value of the securities held.
	Valuation
	Revalued at the end of each day at current prices and exchange rates.
	Assets
CREDIT COOPERATIVES	Foreign currency-denominated bonds may not exceed 20 percent of total securities holdings. Yearly purchases of foreign currency-denominated bonds may not exceed 10 percent of total securities holdings. Bonds only, no equities allowed. Corporate bonds must be rated A or higher. Government bonds must be ranked 20th or higher in the country risk rating published by *Institutional Investor*.

Source: Nomura Securities, Ltd.

Germany as a Marketplace

Christian Watrin

At present, the German economy can be identified as a dual economy. The eastern part, which formerly formed the German Democratic Republic (GDR), is in a thorough and deep structural crisis; whereas, its western part, the former Federal Republic of Germany (FRG), is booming. These highly divergent developments within the political boundaries of one country are the outcome of the dramatic political and economic unification process that occurred in 1990. On March 18, 1990, the former communist government, under the leadership of Hans Modrow, was outvoted by a landslide victory of the newly founded democratic parties. On May 18, 1990, the two Germanys agreed to form an economic, monetary and social union, which commenced on July 1. Shortly afterward, they signed the treaty on the political unification, which came into force on October 3, 1990.

From an economic point of view, the important date was July 1, 1990. On that day, the valueless GDR money was replaced by the deutsche mark, and the two countries practically became one national market. The command economy and its bureaucracy was ousted, the market economy was introduced, and full availability of goods, services, labor and capital was instituted.

Economic Shock Treatment for a Unified Germany

Compared with other examples of economic integration, such as the European integration process or the entry of the small Saarland into the FRG in 1957–59, the establishment of a national market between the two Germanys, from one day to the other, was the most severe shock therapy ever used in recent economic history. It did not take decades, as in the case of the European Community (EC), to approach the aim of forming a single market; neither was there an adjustment period of several years, as in the case of Saarland or when new members joined the EC during the 1970s and 1980s.

The shock therapy led to a situation in which all the inefficiencies of the former centrally administered East German economy suddenly became visible. The highly monopolized firms, the so-called *combinates* [*Kombinate*], and the publicly owned factories now have to compete with the more efficient companies in West Germany and the EC. The situation was aggravated by the conversion rate chosen between the two currencies. For political reasons, the West German government chose a rate of 1-to-1. Eastern companies, previously competing under the protection of a foreign trade monopoly in which their exports were priced on average at 4.6 East German marks for one deutsche mark, now must compete under the conditions of a very sharp revaluation. These companies must lower their prices or increase their productivity dramatically to avoid bankruptcy. Are they likely to survive competition under these new circumstances? Skeptics point to the fact that the quality of many eastern commodities is substandard.[1]

There is little doubt that the productive capacity of nearly all East German companies will have to be restructured in the near future. According to often-cited forecasts, one-third of the companies will have only minor problems in restructuring their production. If capital can be attracted from West German international sources, approximately another 30 percent could be restored to financial soundness. The rest will have to leave the market, which will cause considerable structural unemployment.

The employment situation has been aggravated by wage increases and a sharp fall in labor productivity in the past few months. West German labor unions, eager to recruit members in the East, have put heavy pressure on employers to increase wages without paying much attention to the low productivity of East German workers and the economic situation of their companies.[2]

According to a survey published recently by the five leading West German research institutes, 250,000 workers in East Germany are unemployed and 1.4 million workers are on short-time work, which in many cases is disguised unemployment. For 1991, these institutes forecast that unemployment will increase to 1.4 million and that 1.75 million will be on shorter hours. If this proves to be correct, 40 percent of the total East German work force will be hit by a dramatic slump in employment. Other indicators give further cause for alarm. Labor productivity is low, less than half that of West Germany, and the East German gross national product is shrinking. In 1990, a decrease of 16 percent is anticipated, and despite expectations for an economic upswing in 1991, a further net decrease of 8 percent is estimated.[3] However, this gloomy picture has to be balanced by a more careful interpretation of the unemployment statistics and the benefits of the economic integration already obtained.

A common trait of centrally administered economies is manpower overstaffing, which has two sources. First, the management and workers favor so-called *soft plans*, but both confront a wage system that increases wage payments considerably when plan targets are overfulfilled. Second, the so-called advantage of socialism over capitalism is the job guarantee for all workers, except dissidents, even if their wages are not in line with their productivity or if their contribution to the productive process is zero or negative (as in the case of the intimidating Secret Service). In both cases, the outcome is overmanning, either for the purpose of lessening the pressure of plan fulfillment or of giving in to political pressure. The outcome of a policy of excessive overstaffing, compared with West German firms, is a significant lowering of living standards.[4] Therefore, increases in unemployment must be analyzed from the viewpoint of hidden unemployment and unproductive work in the old command economy. According to an estimate by the *British Weekly Economist*, up to 1.5 million workers out of 8 million fall into this category of unproductive and disguised unemployment.

However, the shock therapy has caused not only harm to the East German economy but also considerable benefits. Consumers have won a new freedom of choice by exchanging their valueless money—the GDR mark—into a world currency, the deutsche mark. Companies that suffered under the communist policy and its inefficiencies now can buy their input from the cheapest competitor in the world market. And in contrast to East European countries, where the transition to a market economy caused high inflation and a slump in real wages, there was neither a price-level increase nor a slowdown of incomes in East Germany. In fact, the consumer price index fell drastically in June 1990 before the monetary and economic union (–12.1 percent compared with June 1989). Since then, despite an increase, the index was still lower in September 1990 than in 1989.

Under the new circumstances, the availability and quality of products is no longer a problem, and consumers do not have to spend endless hours in line for basic foods. Further, instead of a decrease, there has been a considerable increase in real incomes, financed mainly by huge transfer payments from West Germany. And finally, the whole financial structure of West Germany has been introduced into East Germany. The full-fledged commercial bank system has been built up during the past months. All the major West German banks have subsidiaries in the East, and the money supply is under the control of the West German central bank, the *Bundesbank*.

Despite these encouraging developments, an economic upswing in the East, which many hoped would be an immediate outcome of the transition to a market economy and the economic and monetary union with West Germany, did not occur. Nevertheless, many politicians and quite a few economists are convinced that East Germany could become a prosperous market not only for West Germany but also for the EC and the rest of the world. These optimists point to the many entrepreneurially minded people in the East who want to set up their own businesses. If they succeed, labor demand will rise. Also, many West German companies that had subsidiaries or, indeed, their headquarters in the eastern part of the country before 1945 hope to revive their old connections and invest considerable amounts of money to get a new foothold in their former markets.

Further, the West German government, which is now also responsible for the eastern part of the country, has channeled huge funds into the new *Bundesländer* [states] to rebuild the worn out infrastructure, clean up pollution, support social security and finance a deficit of the local and state authorities, which at present have no means necessary to finance their basic requirements.

In thinking along these lines, the European Commission forecasts that West Germany will gain an extra 1 percent of real GNP growth through the economic unification process in the years to come and that the EC as a whole will grow an extra 0.5 percent from German integration. West German economic research institutes are making similar forecasts. The prosperous West German economy, with its annual 3 percent to 4 percent real growth rate, will gain momentum. Like a huge locomotive, the western part of the economy will provide the power to pull out the inefficient and economically small East German economy, which produces only one-tenth of the West German GNP despite a work force that is relatively much larger than West Germany's.

From this widely held view, the main problem is whether a Schumpeterian process of *creative destruction* can be initiated. In other words, will a dynamic growth process overcome the difficulties rising out of the collapse of parts of the eastern economy?

Several preconditions must be fulfilled to close the wealth gap between the eastern and western parts of the recently unified Germany. Property rights must be secured, resource transfers from the West to the East must be financed, and a wage explosion must be avoided.

The Long Road from Socialism to Private Property

Private property is the antithesis of communism and the basis of capitalism.[5] But establishing private property rights now seems to be the most serious problem for initiating a dynamic catch-up process in the former GDR. In the unification treaty, the two governments agreed that property confiscated by the East German government during the past four decades should be returned to the former owners, with the exception of the expropriation initiated by the Soviet military government between 1945 and 1949. From an equity point of view, this policy is just. From an economic point of view, it has the disadvantage that it will impede capital investment by private individuals or banks until property right claims have been settled, which may take many years.

The change of the property rights structure depends not only on property rights to land and buildings but also on how the operating companies will be privatized. Under the former transitional communist government, a giant trust company, the *Treuhandanstalt*, was founded in March 1990. This company is now the legal owner of nearly 8,000 businesses [*Volkseigene Betriebe*], which were under party control in the former communist government. This trusteeship was set up to privatize and, if possible, to restructure East German industry. It has about 1,000 employees, and it is hoped that the trusteeship will be able to sell large parts of East German industry to the public during the next two years.

At present, only 300 companies have been sold off, and the *Treuhandanstalt* has earned 1 billion deutsche marks (approximately $660 million U.S. dollars). The *Treuhandanstalt* has extended large loans to maintain the liquidity of the remaining companies. During the next weeks, the nonprivatized companies must present their opening balances to their new legal owner. Then, the trustees must decide which companies will be restructured and which companies must close. These decisions might cause fierce political debate, and the trustees may be under heavy political pressure to bail out companies that they think are not worthy of financial help. This is one of the main reasons many economists in my country argue for separating the two tasks, namely the selling and the restructuring of the firms, and for the trustees to concentrate solely on the sale of East German industry.

An effective measure would be the introduction of open-tender procedures. The lack of an offer for a company would signal that the market is not ready to absorb it. But the major problems are that the market sets limits on itself and that successful privatizing can proceed only stepwise. If these limits are exceeded, the capital market might collapse.

Financing the Resource Transfer from West Germany to East Germany

West Germany has set up huge public funds to subsidize the East during the next years. According to a preliminary calculation, 100 billion deutsche marks have been spent in 1990, and 120 billion to 150 billion deutsche marks will be spent in 1991. This expenditure will cause heavy deficits in the budget of the central government. Due to big surpluses in the public pension schemes, which can be tapped by the government, the net amount of the overall budget deficit to be financed on the capital market will be only 70 billion deutsche marks in 1990 and 90 billion deutsche marks in 1991.

There are several ways to finance the burden, which in the long run might become a successful investment for the wealth potential of East Germany. West Germany could cut approximately 12 billion deutsche marks ($8 billion U.S. dollars), which were previously used in subsidizing West Berlin, among others, and caused by the division of Germany after World War II. The peace dividend from reduced military expenditures is calculated at another 5 billion to 7 billion deutsche marks ($3 billion to $5 billion U.S. dollars). There is also a chance of reducing the huge subsidies for the European agricultural policy, the inefficient coal industry and the shipyards.

Further, many state-run services could be privatized. For instance, part of the telecommunications monopoly might be a candidate for privatization. Highways could be built by private companies, which would have the right to charge user fees. Parts of the state-owned property could be sold. Also, the *Länder*, which do not contribute much to the financial transfers, could be urged to postpone investments and planned expenditures for several years to help the new German states. And finally, the capital exports of West Germany, which in 1989 were more than 100 billion deutsche marks (approximately $66 billion U.S. dollars), would be channeled into East Germany if the interest rates of state borrowing are attractive.

Large parts of the federal deficit have been financed in 1990 by borrowing on the international financial markets. West Germany, which nearly balanced its overall budget in 1989, ranks on top of the international rating scale. Therefore, the German *Bundesbank* and many government advisers favor further credit financing and reject tax increases. They argue that the deficits rise out of a historically unique situation in which large funds are needed to invest in the East German infrastructure. According to long-held views in economics, such investments should be financed by borrowing and repaid out of future proceeds. The opponents in this debate fear that most of the public money will be spent on consumption and not investment. Therefore, they argue that taxes should be raised for proper financing of the extra burden rising out of the unification process.

Tax increases, however, may be counterproductive under the prevailing circumstances. The top marginal (income tax) rate is already high (53 percent). Its increase could set negative incentives into operation. An increase of indirect taxes—for instance, the value-added tax or the gasoline tax—would depress consumption. Tax increases could be used if financial markets proved to be unwilling to finance further deficits at the prevailing nominal interest rate of 9 percent.

However, the main question is, How will the international financial markets behave? A tight fiscal policy can convince international investors that the

German government has full control of the integration process and that the public budget will be balanced again in a few years.

Wages and Productivity

East German and West German wages were converted 1-to-1 on July 1, 1990. This conversion made imports from West Germany much less expensive than they had been under black-market rates before the monetary union. For the East Germans, this is incentive to buy Western goods and to reject their own, which at current wages are too expensive from their point of view. The outcome, however, is that East Germans are losing the jobs by which they would have produced these goods.

The wage increases during 1990, which on average were 20 percent, have aggravated the employment situation. If further real wage-induced unemployment is to be avoided, future wage policy must be in line with productivity growth. This is the Achilles heel of the whole integration process. In Germany, collective wage agreements play a dominant role even though only one-third of the work force is unionized. The wage demands of the unions—especially the influential public service union, which claims equal pay for equal work—are rising. The equal-pay argument proves to be very powerful because wages in the East are only one-third of those in the West.

It is difficult to forecast how unions will behave in the near future. Protection against dismissal will end in East Germany in mid-1991. The system of redundancy payments has been extended to East Germany. The public debate on the relationship between productivity and employment will be spurred on in the near future. The only way out of the wage trap in which the East German workers are caught now is to increase their productivity quickly. This is not impossible. Experience gained in West Germany after the economic and currency reforms in 1948 show that double-digit increases of productivity are possible at least for some years. This raises hopes that East German workers, who on average know that they will worsen their living standards by demanding excessive wages, will not choose a strategy in which most of them will lose their jobs.

Summary

In summary, Germany as a marketplace is in a much more difficult situation than before political and economic unification occurred. East Germany's run-down economy must be restructured in many parts. At the beginning of this process, the West German economy was in very good condition. Its growth rate was underestimated once more at the beginning of this year. According to recent calculations, real growth will be 4 percent to 4.5 percent. The western part of the economy traditionally has a huge current-account surplus and is the biggest capital exporter in the world after Japan. The budget deficit of the early 1980s was reduced nearly to zero in 1989. The inflation rate is low, and the deutsche mark is one of the strongest currencies in the world.

The economic unification process puts a significant burden on the western part of the economy, but the burden itself seems bearable. The resources transferred to the eastern parts of the country will be *costs* only if they are used to finance consumption there. Therefore, one of the problems to be solved is to channel the bulk of the public transfers into investments, especially investments in the infrastructure of East Germany. If this happens, the East German economy will start to expand and enter the wealth-creating process, which is the normal outcome of an enlarged market.

Notes

1 *Their favorite example is the world's ugliest car, the Trabant. A year ago, East Germans were willing to wait 12 years to 18 years for delivery. Today, nobody will buy it, and the car can be sold only to East European countries with the help of export subsidies that increase consumption in the importing countries at a time when the same funds are sorely needed for investment in the ruined East German economy.*

2 *Employers in the East German context are not employers in a normal sense but are members of the old party elite, which ruined the country. Therefore, their opposition to wage increases is not very strong; on the contrary, many of them hope to keep their privileged positions by not resisting wage demands.*

3 *The East German GNP in 1990 is approximately 243.5 billion deutsche marks ($162.3 billion U.S. dollars). The estimate for 1991 is 232 billion deutsche marks ($154.5 billion U.S. dollars).*

4 *One example is given by the East German Railways. They employ the same number of workers as the West German Bundesbahn (240,000) but serve a railway system that is only one-fourth as large as the one in the West. The same holds true for universities, broadcasting companies, research institutes and the big firms.*

5 *N. Colchester,* The Economist, *June 30, 1990.*

Prospects for a U.S.–Mexico Free Trade Agreement: Lessons from Canada

James R. Markusen

Let me begin by confessing that despite the title of this speech, I certainly am not an expert on Mexico. I began research on a possible U.S.–Mexico agreement, especially with respect to automobiles, but I am very far from an expert and hope I do not get too many embarrassing questions. What I have done largely by accident, I think, is make a career of living in places that are undergoing significant trade liberalizations or of living there shortly afterward. I come here having spent about 18 years in Canada, during which time there was a tremendous amount of trade liberalizations in goods, services and investment policies of Canada. I was fortunate to spend two years in Australia and New Zealand, one of which was before liberalization occurred in the early 1980s (1980–81). I was able to return for a second year, 1987–88, after substantial changes had occurred in both countries, particularly in New Zealand. Two years ago, I was lucky enough to spend six months in Israel, which had just had major reforms both to domestic policies and to its international trade exchange rate and monetary policies.

So, in some sense, I am a professional liberalization watcher, and I try to see how the results of these liberalizations conform or fail to conform to various economic theories and predictions that we make.

Today, I will proceed in three steps. First, I will describe two broad conceptual models, or perhaps we could call them theories of international trade, and the consequences of trade liberalization as viewed from the perspective of these models. The models have very different implications, and they are in the background as policymakers and others draw scenarios about possible outcomes of free trade. Thus, it is important to try to shed light on the models from actual experience because they are very different.

Second, I will relate the actual experiences of U.S.–Canada trade liberalization to these conceptual models and ask, Which theory seems to fit best, and for what types of industry do they seem to fit best?

Finally, I will relate the U.S.–Canada experience to the possibility of U.S.–Mexico trade liberalization, the possible effects of that liberalization on both countries and perhaps make some speculative comments about the political process that may or may not cause substantial liberalization. So, I am trying to use the actual experience from Canada to shed some light on the unknown questions about the United States and Mexico.

First, the conceptual models. I will call the first model the *comparative advantage view of international trade.* This model, which goes back to David Ricardo, is almost 200 years old and has long been the mainstay of courses in international trade theory. (David Ricardo was one of the few economic theorists ever to become rich on the stock market, so he has always had a special place in my heart. He was a very good practical man as well as a good theorist.) In this view, countries are inherently good at producing certain kinds of goods and services, and they are inherently bad, or high-cost, producers of other goods and services. These relative abilities, or what Ricardo called *comparative advantage,* are in turn related to underlying features of economies. In particular, factor endowments have received the most attention. So in this view, we would see Mexico as a labor-abundant country, and we would see the United States as abundant in capital in all its forms—physical capital, human capital and knowledge capital—and those in turn create relative differences in the ability to produce goods and services cheaply.

Trade liberalization in this comparative advantage view leads countries to specialize more in those goods that use intensively their abundant factors. So in the comparative advantage view, U.S.–Mexico trade liberalization would lead the United States to specialize more in activities intensive in physical, human and knowledge capital and to contract production of labor-intensive activities. Mexico would do the opposite, expanding labor-intensive production and exporting those goods to the United States. So in this view, there are substantial interindustry shifts. The United States will be good in some industries and bad in others; the former expand and the latter contract as a consequence of trade liberalization.

The comparative advantage view has direct implications for returns to factors of production, particularly labor, of concern to the United States. With unskilled or perhaps semiskilled labor, the comparative advantage view sees differences in wage levels in a protected market as a reflection of factor endowment. So in this view, the United States has high wages because it is a labor-scarce country, and Mexico has low wages because it is a labor-abundant country. With trade liberalization, the wages are pulled together by integrating economies; in some sense, the United States becomes less labor-scarce and Mexico becomes less labor-abundant. The wage rates are pulled together, so you expect that U.S. wages will fall for this class of workers and Mexican wages will rise. Last, the comparative advantage model emphasizes bilateral trade creation, and this is something we try to stress in economics. There is a tendency for many commentators on trade liberalization to focus excessively on import penetration and its effects on the economy, and they spend a much smaller percentage of their time commenting on export expansion and the beneficiaries from that expansion.

Overall, the comparative advantage view of the world can leave you with serious reservations about free trade between Mexico and the United States. While this view says that U.S. gross national product (GNP) may increase, it also says that the increase may be very unevenly distributed and that there may be a lot of cost. To certain groups, the comparative advantage view suggests the possible contraction of labor-intensive manufacturing in the United States. It suggests the possibility of a substantial fall in wages for unskilled and semiskilled workers in the United States, and it suggests substantial adjustment costs for workers, firms and, to some extent, regions insofar as certain industries are concentrated in certain regions. For example, textiles, clothing and furniture are concentrated in the Southeast. This uneven distribution of the gains from trade is an inherent feature of the comparative advantage view of the world, and as such, it can lead to very legitimate questions as to whether or not an increase in GNP is worth the uneven distribution of those gains across groups within society and possibly across regions. Many of these ideas, I think, are reflected by commentators on trade, whether they explicitly have learned this model in a course in international trade, or it has rubbed off. We certainly see these comments in several of the discussions.

Let me turn to the second model, which I will call the *industrial organization model.* This model is more recent in international trade theory, but in fact it actually goes back to Adam Smith, who had his ideas later relegated to the backwater. The industrial organization model tends to focus much more on individual firms and individual industries and the interdependence among firms in the industry. Key factors in the industrial organization approach are increasing returns to scale both in production and to research and development activity; larger markets support increased production, which allows you to spread fixed costs of capital more finely across output and fixed costs of research and development more finely across a product, thereby lowering the average cost of those investments. The industrial organization view stresses the role of specialization by plant and by firm in producing high productivity and efficient production. The industrial organization model stresses the role of product differentiation in two ways: the larger market supports a larger number of products, which increases consumer welfare and also a larger range of intermediate products and services. The larger markets support more specialization, both in physical inputs and in knowledge inputs, such as consulting services that increase the efficiency of production.

A very important feature of the industrial organization view, to contrast the comparative advantage view, is the industrial organization view sees differences in scale and technological and organizational sophistication as being a major determinate of wage differences across the country. So in this view, the notion that the United States is a high-wage country simply because it is labor-scarce and Mexico is a low-wage country simply because it is labor-abundant is at best a small part of the story.

A great deal of the productivity difference is caused by technology, organization scale and other advantages in the United States. It is even well understood that if we physically transported a plant from the United States to Mexico, that by even duplicating the physical facilities, one does not get the same output from that plant. As a consequence of this observation, there is no strong presumption in the industrial organization model that trade liberalization will lower the wages in a high-wage country. As I indicated a moment ago, the comparative advantage approach sees trade liberalization as pulling wage levels together because they are caused only by differences in relative labor scarcity. The industrial organization view sees wage differences as caused by other factors, and it is entirely possible that because of increases in scale and specialization and the profitability of research and development that trade liberalization can, in fact, raise wages in the larger markets. This is one of the key differences between the two approaches for analyzing U.S.–Mexico trade.

The industrial organization model sees tremendous scope for rationalization at the firm and the plant level. Plants become more specialized, some product lines or components are dropped from individual plants, but other product components are produced in larger batches for a larger world market. Intra-industry trade increases as plants and firms become more specialized, producing smaller numbers of products or components, exporting larger portions of their batches and importing those products that are no longer produced within that same plant. Thus, we expect a lot of intra-industry and intrafirm adjustment in the industrial organization approach as opposed to the interindustry adjustment that is predicted by the comparative advantage approach.

The industrial organization approach sees the burden falling less on individual groups like skilled or unskilled labor and less on the individual regions but perhaps more on individual firms that simply cannot measure up to a more competitive, larger environment. Both the industrial organization approach and the competitive model emphasize export expansion along with import penetration.

Canadian Experience Coincides with the Industrial Organization View

Returning to the Canadian experience, I want to quickly review the period 1970 to 1990. There was tremendous trade liberalization during this period; tariffs fell by more than half. A lot of quantitative controls were dismantled, and foreign investment policies were substantially liberalized within the past five years. The Auto Pact of 1967 created free trade in automobiles. In 1970, Canada was worried about severe damage to its manufacturing sector by trade liberalization. In that sense, Canada's position was similar to that of some U.S. manufacturing industries today that are worried about the possible effects of competition in labor-intensive activities from Mexico. The worry in Canada was that there would be a revision to a resource-based economy. We were going to be hewers of wood and drawers of water, which is an old Canadian phrase, although I was politely told in Israel that this phrase was from the book of Kings, much to the surprise of most Canadians.

So, the worry in Canada was about this large interindustry shift, that the manufacturing sector would be devastated, and we would go back to being farmers and lumberjacks—a nation of McKenzie brothers, more or less. This view is consistent with the comparative advantage model, which suggests that you are either good or bad at certain activities, and trade liberalization will weed out the bad ones and leave you to specialize in the good ones.

Well, what were the results? The results of trade liberalization for Canada are that the industrial organization model was a much better predictor of what actually happened than the comparative advantage theory. In Canada, there were relatively small interindustry shifts in production. Canadians did not close manufacturing industries and revert to being farmers and lumberjacks. There was very little of that as a percentage of all changes in activity. There were, on the other hand, large rationalizations at industry and firm levels. We got very good data on these things in Canada. We found firms producing longer production runs, larger plants and fewer products per plant. Canada had net exit of firms and consolidation of firms and industries so that it wound up with fewer, stronger, larger, more efficient firms than it had at the beginning of the time period. Labor movement among sectors, like the movement in production, was very small. Basically, manufacturing workers stayed in the manufacturing sector, which was rationalizing, and did not move to the farm or to the forest. A study for the McDonald Commission, which preceded the decision in Canada to seek a free trade agreement, found that about 90 percent of labor adjustment in Canada during the 1970s had nothing to do with trade liberalization, but it had to do with other factors involving changes in technology, changes in consumer preferences, new products and so forth. The study found that trade liberalization resulted in a very small percentage movement in labor among sectors.

The Canadian experience tends to confirm the view that differences in wage rates are not simply a result of labor abundance or scarcity, but they reflect underlying real productivity differences stemming from technology, organization, scale and other factors. Canada, entering the period with significantly lower real manufacturing wages than the United States, hardly swamped the United States with cheap manufactured goods. Instead, there was a very large, two-way increase in manufacturing and trade between the two countries. Both exports and imports increased in real terms by about 40 percent during the 1970s, which again suggests this rationalization of producing fewer products, longer production runs and so forth.

The bottom line for Canada was that trade liberalization resulted in significant rationalization within sectors and very little intersectorial shift.

What the U.S.–Canada Experience Implies for Mexico

What are the implications for Mexico? I think there has been too much worry about wage differentials. Wage differentials, as the Canadian experience suggests, are not just labor abundance. They are a reflection of organization, technology and other factors. One statistic—that U.S. industrial wages may be five times those of Mexico—is very misleading and is sometimes used to argue that some U.S. sectors may be wiped out. Those wage differences are endogenous. They are determined by productivity differences, and those productivity differences will not disappear on the advent of free trade. There are legitimate worries about certain low-wage, labor-intensive production activities.

Here, I would like to point out what others have said. They have pointed out that the diversion of jobs from the United States in these activities may not be from the United States to Mexico, but they might be from Asia to Mexico. U.S. firms have been shedding certain activities, rationalizing their activities, for some years now and will continue to do so, indeed they will have to do so quite independently of a possible U.S.–Mexico agreement. The Mexican option to locate certain activities in Mexico may, in fact, be crucial to help some U.S. firms survive and provide high-quality jobs in the United States.

Mattel said in the *New York Times* over the weekend that if there is a U.S.–Mexico trade agreement, it will move a substantial number of jobs of manufacturing toys to Mexico, but they will not come from the United States; they will come from Asia. The jobs will come from production facilities or subcontractors currently located in the Far East, not from the United States.

Germany, in some ways, did something closely related with its guest worker system. The idea there was that it is very valuable for the industry to have access to a pool of low-wage workers to support the profitability and competitiveness of the German firms and provide high-quality jobs for nationals. In a sense, free trade for the United States could be thought of as somewhat similar to the guest worker system, except the workers are not guests; they get to stay in their own country, and components, parts or final products are shipped across the border between the United States and Mexico.

The Canadian experience suggests that there is much more scope for intrafirm and intra-industry adjustment than I think a lot of people fear. I can see firms shedding products or parts and increasing production of others for a larger market—that is, rationalizing within plants instead of shutting down firms. Being able to locate certain labor-intensive activities in Mexico, the U.S. firms can increase their competitiveness, which is very important today. This is exactly what Japan is doing in Southeast Asia, where it has relocated a tremendous amount of production. The view in Japan, as I understand it, is that Japan will be the brains and Southeast Asia will be the brawn to a lot of the low-wage, relatively low-skill, labor-intensive activity. And in a sense, that is what the United States would be doing with the U.S.–Mexico trade agreement.

Finally, I would like to emphasize the export potential. It is enormous, and it has been growing. This is not a matter of guesswork. The Mexican liberalizations of the past few years have resulted in U.S. exports to Mexico doubling in five years. Exports are now about $30 billion and have increased more than in proportion to U.S. imports from Mexico. Mexican liberalization has led to large percentage increases in the imports of both final and intermediate goods. I have seen one estimate that suggests that 15 percent of every $1 increase in Mexican income will be spent on U.S. products. Observers assert that the equivalent figure for the Far East is far smaller and, in fact, is close to zero.

In other words, a U.S.–Mexico agreement that relocated production activities from the Far East to Mexico will have a substantial positive effect on U.S. export sales to Mexico.

I will conclude with a couple of brief political comments. From the Canadian point of view, free trade with the United States was inconceivable 10 years ago. I think it was even out of the question five years ago. What happened in Canada was that as Canadians gained experience, especially increased experience in doing business abroad, firms in Canada became more aware of the possibility of rationalization, more aware of export possibilities and less preoccupied with the notion of import penetration, which is only one side of the two-sided coin of trade liberalization. Canadian firms became more confident in their abilities. One of the unknowns in the current situation on both sides of the U.S.–Mexico border is presumably the same thing. Will firms see the opportunities for rationalization and export in a larger market, or will they focus narrowly on the possibility of losses, given their existing product lines and their existing limited domestic market? And this, I suspect, is a key question.

The Mexicans today, from my experience, are strongly committed to the change. I think it is genuine, I think it is permanent. It pervades the ruling party in Mexico. I am fairly sure I know what the Mexicans are thinking and what their objectives are, and I think they are very genuine in what they say. Ironically, I am far less clear about what the U.S. government is thinking. I am not at all sure I know what the administration is thinking, what its motives are and where it wants to end up. This may simply be the consequence of the fact that Mexico is focusing narrowly on well-defined economic goals, whereas the U.S. position is a muddle of economics, politics and global trade strategy. But insofar as I do not understand exactly what the U.S. government is thinking, I have very little idea how to predict the success or failure of further liberalization.

PART THREE

Investing in the Future

"This North Texas region, I believe, will be the fastest-growing part of the country for the next 10 to 15 years. A lot of it will have to do with the work we did in North Texas in the past three to four years building this great foundation."

—Ross Perot, Jr.

"[I]f we do not do better about seeing that our research is used by American industry, we will find that our excellent research is subsidizing our competitors' industrial base far more effectively than it is supporting our own."

—Keren K. Ware

"Until now, the country has been hamstrung.... The obvious solution. ...would be to get rid of the federal grants. Let the community put up a toll gate or airport fee, and outsiders using that facility will pay the fee like anybody else."

—Edward M. Gramlich

"In this state, we have tiptoed through a minefield of political problems for many years. I really think that if we do not solve the financing problem, someone else will do it for us."

—Dan W. Cook, III

Making the Future Work

Ross Perot, Jr.

In 1983, The Perot Group began to develop the last remaining quadrant of the Dallas/Fort Worth Metroplex, an area of 4 million people. We currently own 16,000 acres in this quadrant, with 10,000 acres in active development. This regional development includes

- The 4,800-acre Alliance Center, with Alliance Airport at its core.
- Alliance Gateway, a 2,500-acre development bisected by State Highway 170.
- Two residential projects—the Villages of Park Glen—which provide affordable housing for the people who work in the Alliance region.

Along with other developers, these three projects will build the last remaining piece of the Dallas/Fort Worth Metroplex.

What Can Private Enterprise Do to Help Get This Project off the Ground?

The Alliance project began in early 1987 when the Federal Aviation Administration (FAA) asked us to donate land for an airport. We had a 2,500-acre piece of property with rail service on the west side and freeway service on the east. We said, "All right. We will donate land for an airport. How long will it take you to build it?" The FAA said, "Well, it will take eight to 10 years." This is a very significant point in the whole conversation, and it really set the tone for what we are trying to do. We said, "All right. What can private enterprise do to help public enterprise get this project off the ground? Can we form a public–private partnership to make this airport happen more quickly?"

The FAA said that if we wanted to, we could use private dollars for the engineering and environmental work and to handle the zoning and annexation of the property. In effect, private funding could build the whole package for the Alliance project, give that package to the city of Fort Worth, and then the city of Fort Worth and the FAA would build the airport. We said, "Fine. We'll do that."

The FAA also said that if they did not approve the airport we would lose our investment. We said, "Well, we understand that. Now we want you (the city of Fort Worth and the FAA) to dedicate a team of people we can work with every week. So as we go through this program every week, we will know that we are doing the right thing."

To make a long story short, 18 months after the FAA came to us, Alliance Airport broke ground. When Alliance broke ground, it was five times larger than what the FAA first envisioned. When it broke ground, it was the only industrial airport to be built in the United States at that time. It was also the fastest airport that the FAA has built, and it was the largest new airport to be built in the United States since D/FW Airport opened in 1974. It became a major airport program for the FAA and a model for other large infrastructure projects around the United States.

In addition to Alliance Airport, we wanted to be sure we had a good freeway system through the market and that we could link Alliance Airport and D/FW Airport. Alliance Airport is only 15 nautical miles northwest of D/FW Airport. Using the same Alliance philosophy—the teamwork philosophy—we began to work with the highway department. The highway department wanted to build a road in the area because there was public need. You must have public need for these kinds of projects. We bought an additional 2,500 acres of property and donated land for the new freeway, along with the Circle T ranch and IBM. IBM has a 1,000-acre campus in this region. So, of the 18-mile outer loop linking these two airports, 13 miles were donated to the highway department, plus the engineering and environmental work. That freeway is now under construction.

The third piece of the project is the residential phase. We realized that when we started these big commercial projects, it would not only generate a tremendous amount of jobs but would also generate a tremendous demand for housing. We wanted to be sure that we could capture that market. We bought 3,500 acres and could then build more than 8,000 houses. These houses had to be affordable so the people who worked at the airport and on the freeway could afford to live there. Few large cities in the country have an affordable supply of quality housing close to future job centers.

The first phase of the residential project broke ground 18 months ago. Today, we have sold more than 300 houses in Park Glen. Typical home prices range between $80,000 and $90,000. Park Glen is a community with a new park system, church, day care center and elementary school; it is a master-planned community. All the landscaping is in and, for $80,000, it is probably the finest home bargain now in the North Texas marketplace. In these past 18 months, Park Glen has become the fastest-growing community in Tarrant County and the second fastest-growing community in North Texas. So that program is progressing well.

Alliance Airport, as I mentioned earlier, has rail service on the west side, a new airport in the middle and freeway service on the east side. Three modes of transportation are feeding this project, which has grown from 2,500 acres to 4,800 acres. We have continued to buy property around Alliance because we realize that most of our customers need 100 to 200 acres, and we want to be sure this airport can continue to grow and meet the economic development reasons for which it was built. Alliance can handle any type of rail, air or interstate customer, so we market from the commercial through the industrial realm of users.

Who Uses Alliance Airport?

The largest user at Alliance currently is American Airlines. American purchased 277 acres at Alliance and built a $600 million maintenance base. That facility opened in one year. The American Airlines facility, with six towers taller than 165 feet, is the largest cantilever hanger complex in the world. It will accommodate seven jumbo jets in one building at the same time. It is a huge facility. This complex will employ 4,500 people and will open by the end of 1991. American will first maintain 757s, then 767s and then the airbus.

The second-largest user is Santa Fe Railway. Santa Fe purchased 55 acres at Alliance, with Honda and Ford as their two main customers. They built an auto-distribution center and move 130,000 cars per year through this site. That facility opened three or four months ago.

The third-largest user is The Ishida Group. They are building a new tilt-wing aircraft at Alliance, the TW-68. This airplane will take off like a helicopter and fly like an airplane. Their research and development facilities are being built today. Their production facilities will be built within the next 18 to 20 months. This airplane will revolutionize travel, much like the tilt-rotor aircraft that Bell Helicopter is now developing. It is exciting that both the tilt-rotor and the tilt-wing are being developed in this marketplace. Both of them should be very successful and employ thousands of people for many years to come.

The fourth-largest user is the Drug Enforcement Agency. They will build their new air wing at Alliance, employing roughly 150 people. Their building will be 200,000 feet, and they will maintain 92 aircraft at Alliance.

If you look at the Ishida family, Mr. Ishida is the grandson of the founder of Toyota. He is the largest single stockholder left in Toyota, and he spent 20 years working for Toyota before he left to start this new aviation company. He has the experience and the financial power to build the aircraft, which is truly an international aircraft. Its components will be coming from around the world to Texas. By the end of this century, you should probably see 2,000 to 3,000 people working at Alliance Airport building these new tilt-wing aircraft. It will carry 10 to 15 people and will cost $4 million to $5 million. So, in that price range, it will revolutionize highway travel, be extremely affordable, and there should be a tremendous demand for that product.

The fifth-largest user at Alliance Airport is the FAA. They moved their Flight Standards District Office to Alliance in September 1990.

The formal opening of Alliance Airport was in December 1989. We have roughly 16,000 takeoffs and landings each month at Alliance and will have 200,000 operations this year. That estimate is 10 years ahead of what the FAA predicted when this airport broke ground.

From an aviation standpoint, Alliance has been a great success. From an industrial standpoint, keeping American Airlines in Texas was a great success. Without an industrial airport like Alliance, North Texas probably would have lost American Airlines.

Looking at other activity around the project, we now have three interchanges on Interstate 35 West under construction that will open in the spring of 1992. On the freeway yesterday, we held the groundbreaking ceremonies for the new food distribution center for Food Lion. Food Lion is building a 123-acre site, a 1.2 million square-foot facility. Food Lion is now the strongest grocery store company in the United States, and they are moving into the Texas market. Food Lion will build 40 new grocery stores in this market over the next 12 months, with another 40 stores to follow. So, within two years, 80 new grocery stores will enter this market. And if you look at their track record in other parts of the country, because of their quality and their ability to run their business, they probably will lower food prices $100 per year for every man, woman and child in the North Texas market. That should have a tremendous impact on the consumer. They have already bought half their store sites, and they will start breaking ground for those stores in a few weeks. They are a great anchor tenant for our freeway program and also a great company to have moving into the Texas market, beginning in North Texas.

Let's look at the other activity on this freeway. IBM has a new facility between D/FW Airport and Alliance Airport. They built more than 2 million square feet between the airports and employ 4,000 people at that facility. Marriott Hotels opened a new hotel there this summer. Club Corporation of America is now building new health facilities. In effect, an entire community is being built for IBM. IBM will have 6 million square feet at this complex and 15,000 people by the mid-1990s—a huge job center for this part of the Metroplex.

Mobile Land Corp. purchased 1,400 acres in June 1990 and is now beginning a residential project in the area. Arvita, from Florida, purchased 300 acres and is building a residential project. Tandy Computers opened a new facility in north Fort Worth two years ago. The U.S. Treasury built a new currency facility in Fort Worth that will open in early 1991. They will print $1 bills. Burlington Northern is the newest user in the market. Two or three weeks ago they bought the

Western Center complex and will move their training division into the north Fort Worth market. Marriott has Fossil Creek in the region; Motorola and Coca-Cola are its two anchor tenants. So, many large land developers are moving into the market, as are the big users.

This part of Dallas/Fort Worth is the fastest-growing part of the Metroplex. With the infrastructure, water, sewer, roads, interchanges and fiber optics all going in at one time, all the industrial and commercial activity is happening at once. In the past three years, there has been a tremendous amount of activity that will allow North Texas to continue to grow.

When you look at the numbers, this area should have another 1 million to 1.5 million people by 2005 to 2010. Most of these people will move to the Metroplex not only because of the jobs being created, but also because of the affordability of the land. We are one of the few areas in the country today that have all the infrastructure to compete for any type of industrial activity. The only thing we now cannot compete for in North Texas is a facility that needs a seaport. And if we could figure out how to get a seaport here, we might try it. But, we haven't worked out that one yet.

We are fortunate because these are truly national competitions, and we now have everything needed to win. This North Texas region, I believe, will be the fastest-growing part of the country for the next 10 to 15 years. A lot of it will have to do with the work we did in North Texas in the past three to four years building this great foundation.

Four Competitive Advantages for North Texas

Obviously, I think the future is very bright. There are four good reasons.

Number One: We have a very good water supply in North Texas that will last until 2030. Very few of our competing cities have water that will last that long. Our water supply will attract many industrial users.

Number Two: We have an outstanding freeway system. We are building new freeways around the Metroplex today. Compared with the East Coast or the West Coast, we have a very good road system, and again, that will attract more and more people.

Number Three: We now have the finest airport system in the United States—probably the finest airport system in the world. D/FW Airport, currently the second-busiest airport in the world, should become the busiest airport in the world by 2000. The FAA built Alliance Airport because they wanted to start building a series of reliever airports around D/FW Airport so that D/FW can literally double in capacity during the next 10 to 15 years. Alliance Airport will handle the industrial growth and relieve D/FW of its cargo operation, so that as

D/FW continues to grow, it can be truly dedicated to moving people. Alliance is the backroom operation for a giant airport like D/FW.

Activity continues around airports: two new runways at D/FW Airport, the new Alliance Airport, the new Spinks Airport that opened two years ago in south Fort Worth and the McKinney Airport, which the FAA is now building in the northeast part of the Metroplex (that will be completed within a year). The FAA also will build a new airport by the super collider in the near future.

So, four new airports have developed around D/FW Airport in the past two to three years, making this the finest airport system in the country. We must continue to support our airports and do everything we can to increase aviation capacity, because aviation is key to our economy. The D/FW Metroplex is the third-largest aviation center in the United States, ranking behind Seattle and Los Angeles. By 2000, we probably will be the largest aviation center in the United States, because we still have adequate airport capacity to grow, and we still have the work force that can handle this growth.

Seattle no longer has the ability to attract the workers for continued growth; they have pretty well topped out. Los Angeles, because of the environmental and cost-of-living problems, has now seen aviation companies leave the area for other parts of the United States. Los Angeles will begin to drop. Because of our capacity, we will become the largest aviation center in the country. We have the infrastructure in place, and we must be sure it continues to grow.

Number Four: The final reason North Texas is competitive is just the attitude of the people here. We have a very positive attitude. I realize that this is truly a Dallas/Fort Worth speech and I should talk a little about Houston, but if I am in Houston I change it a little bit. The attitude of people in North Texas—and Houston—has been very positive, and Houston has done a fabulous job. A lot of the things that I am talking about can also apply to Houston, with their great roads and airport system.

People work together in Texas. If you look at what we have done throughout this recession, when times are really tough, we continue to move forward. Some of our greatest economic development victories have occurred during this recession, starting with JCPenney, which moved from Manhattan three or four years ago. Then GTE moved their facilities to North Texas, and Fujitsu announced their factory in North Texas. MCI moved from Washington to North Texas. The super collider was announced, and Exxon announced last year that they are moving their headquarters to North Texas. American Airlines announced their project at Alliance. Burlington Northern moved their headquarters to Fort Worth.

You have seen all these great companies move here to take advantage of the team spirit and the attitude. Tom Smith, chairman of Food Lion, builds grocery stores all around the country. He said that this is absolutely the best business environment in the United States, and it is very important for us to maintain it. He said building permits are faster, the city officials wanted to work with him, and they broke ground almost 10 to 11 days after they closed on the property. Smith said that it takes 18 months to two years to build a warehouse in Florida with their approval process. He said, "Ross, you keep that attitude, you keep the business and the public working together, and more and more companies will come here just because it is a great place to do business, an easy place to do business, and because North Texas wants their business." We must keep that positive attitude. If we keep that attitude, our future will be very bright.

Business Development from R&D to Innovation

Keren K. Ware

We are beginning a decade that promises to be as different from the 1980s as the 20th century has been different from the 19th.

The morning's speakers talked about our nation's shifting global alliances and our international relationships in a rapidly changing political scene. But their analysis of new international relationships and an increasingly interdependent global economy raises another issue—one that will also define this decade—and that is the issue of economic competitiveness. What will be our nation's place in the new global order as it takes shape? Will the United States continue to be an economic leader? Can we remain political leaders? What kinds of jobs will our children have? Will they work for themselves, for Americans, or for someone else? Will it even matter whom they work for?

There are many well-worn aspects to the question of economic competitiveness—education and training, capital, infrastructure and others—and others on this panel will touch on some of them. My focus will be on technological competitiveness and, specifically, on our ability to take the world-class research and development of our universities, our federal and corporate labs, our small businesses and consortia, and to get it fully realized in the marketplace.

I do not want to belabor all the gee-whiz statistics that we have heard on our flagging technological competitiveness. We are now fully accustomed to talking about research breakthroughs and Nobel Prizes in the same breath that we talk about flagging market share in yet another high-technology industry. It's in the newspaper every day.

We are right to pride ourselves on our fine research. However, if we do not do better about seeing that our research is used by American industry, we will find that our excellent research is subsidizing our competitors' industrial base far more effectively than it is supporting our own.

In the following pages, I will touch on the challenges Texas and American companies face in using our own research—challenges representing both macro- and microeconomic barriers to technological competitiveness. Then I will share some examples and insights from community leaders in Texas who are addressing these barriers in practical and effective ways.

Barriers to U.S. Technological Competitiveness

Earlier this year, the Texas Department of Commerce created a product development task force. The task force reviewed the barriers faced by companies, particularly by small businesses, that were attempting to bring new technology-based products and processes into the marketplace. We found several. The first barrier was quickly apparent; it has to do with capital constraints. These constraints include the cost of capital in this country vis-a-vis the cost for competitors in Japan and Western Europe, the pressures for a short-term return thus induced in many American capital providers, and the actual capital shortages.

For example, venture capital has shifted away from early-stage financing toward financing larger, later-stage deals, such as mergers, acquisitions and leveraged buyouts. Venture capitalists are no longer doing the technology startups that we tend to think of when we think of the venture capital community. More traditional financial institutions in Texas and around the country are retrenching. They are largely unwilling or unable to finance projects that depend on introducing new, untried products—even if the borrower is an operating company that has good management, experience in the industry and a good track record.

Another set of barriers is related to corporate culture. These are very American problems, such as a preference among our scientists for theoretical research over applied science. Another example is the famous "not invented here" mentality—the "NIH syndrome" that is a holdover from the days when U.S. companies set the pace of innovation for the rest of the world. Our scientists and engineers are often unwilling to look outside their own laboratories for solutions. A third cultural barrier results from American management systems, in which our corporations—especially our larger corporations, the engineering, marketing and manufacturing operations—tend not to communicate with each other very well.

These capital and cultural barriers are broad-based national and regional problems affecting a variety of companies in fairly global ways. Other barriers we identified are related to the management and information needs of a particular company, needs that are specific to a business seeking financing for a particular project. For example, although they may have a very promising new product line, many engineering-based companies—companies built around a technology or a new invention—may not have the full complement of expertise or information to address the new technology concerns or to address global markets. Market information for untried projects is difficult to access and very hard to evaluate. Then there are a whole host of regulatory issues, international standards and intellectual property problems that can destroy a new product introduction if the legal implications are neglected or misunderstood.

In short, the task force found a lot of powerful, quantifiable reasons not to venture into new product development and not to risk bringing forward an innovative new process or product. As a nation, in fact, we have become very good at measuring the cost of action—what we risk by doing a deal—but we have no means of accounting for the consequences of inaction, of not pursuing a new technology or a new market. We are unable to measure the damage done by that kind of accounting...until we see the statistics of lost market share, of lost businesses, of entire industries that have been displaced by an exciting new product or a revolutionary manufacturing change or manufacturing technique developed elsewhere.

Why are these barriers so powerful? If we categorize them a little differently, we see that there are macroeconomic pressures that bias the markets against any sort of long-term investment in technology, and there are very specific, very critical microeconomic issues that may plague a particular company with a particular deal or transaction. My sense about the policy discussion on technological competitiveness is that we have become almost completely preoccupied with the first set of problems—the macroeconomic forces—to the neglect of some of the challenges on which we can have more impact.

It does make pretty good cocktail party talk—railing about the cost of capital, what the federal government should do. "If the federal government would just reduce the national debt or increase the national savings rate or change the tax structure or free our financial institutions, then," the story goes, "the financial markets could start to work properly, market forces would go to work, and this region and this nation would start investing in the future again, making the investments in productivity and innovation that will keep us on a competitive track with our trading partners." These are all valid points. They sound good, and no one at the cocktail party is ever going to wave his drink, call your bluff, and say, "Okay. I will lower the cost of capital. Will you make that investment?"

An overemphasis on macro issues permits us to blame the administration, to blame Washington, the Fed, the Japanese, whoever our favorite villain is, for all our competitiveness problems and causes us to miss some significant opportunities for technology development. In short, we have forgotten the second half of the adage, "Think globally, act locally."

Community Models Promoting Technological Competitiveness

I would like to spend the rest of my time on some very particular microeconomic barriers to product development and the corresponding particular transaction-oriented ways some community leaders in Texas are addressing this competitiveness issue.

Favorable tax policy, lower capital costs and better capitalized banks are certainly needed, but alone they will not solve the technological competitiveness problem. We cannot afford to wait for macro policy to change, and we cannot assume that macroeconomic changes will solve our problems. We need instead to be proactive today, addressing the problems we can solve one company, one opportunity at a time.

After all, microeconomics is where the rubber hits the road. No company has ever been turned down for a loan for an investment by a "market force." Companies are turned down one at a time by a banker, by an investor, by potential corporate partners. Often, the problem is not an overly high level of risk; it is not the restrictive cost of capital, but it is the hidden costs of the specific transaction. By hidden costs, I mean the time, money and expertise needed to assess the technology investment: costs of acquiring objective technical reviews of the company's technology, reasonably logical market assessments and legal and accounting expertise for what may be somewhat atypical financial arrangements. These are the hidden costs of making a technology investment, and they will always be higher than for a comparable low-tech, no-innovation opportunity.

If markets operate efficiently, then the invisible hand will always be a little arthritic about delivering the technology-investment dollar. The easier deal—oil, real estate, retail—will always be done first. My challenge as an economic developer, and I hope your challenge as leaders concerned about the vitality of your local communities, is to find ways to make the new technology investment, and other productive investments, easier to do.

How do we do this? There are ways to address these hidden costs. Community programs that make it easier for local sources of capital to make investments in technological projects that will benefit their communities. It is interesting how effective local efforts to promote technology and investments appear to be. In fact, their effectiveness probably derives from their being local. I will describe three model projects that are operating today. They are operating in very different communities and drawing on very different kinds of community resources.

The first model is the Austin Technology Incubator. ATI was created by key business and university leaders to create a focal point in Austin for the delivery of a great deal of time and expertise to a specific target—a small number of young, high-technology companies that were judged to have great potential for commercial success. The incubator program did not have money, but it could offer some space. The program had a very strong, committed board of directors as a hook, and they tapped university faculty for technical assistance. ATI has drawn on the Austin professional community for legal and accounting expertise and has developed relationships with bankers, private investors and potential corporate partners on behalf of ATI tenants.

In its first year, the incubator reviewed more than 350 business plans, assisted and advised many of those companies and then selected those that best fit the program's goals and capabilities, those whom it could assist the most. The incubator drew on the university expertise, the local business expertise and the connections and experience of its board, and it has added real value and credibility to these eight or 10 companies.

Assessing any kind of program such as this is very hard. The incubator is now about 15 months old, and these programs take a long time to develop. But in its first 12 months, it created 130 jobs and attracted $10 million in investment to participating companies. Those are remarkable achievements on a budget of $125,000.

The second model is a little different. While Austin is widely regarded as a high-tech community, with a potent concentration of resources, our second example is in Tyler. While Tyler does not have one of the state's leading research universities, the Tyler Economic Development Council recognized the role that their University of Texas Health Science Center could play. Community leaders concluded that they could create a focal point for the medical instrumentation industry in Tyler. They chose to focus on that economic development niche and pursue medical instrumentation opportunities.

They persuaded the local industrial foundation to establish a small seed capital fund, about $200,000. The council set up another revolving loan program using community development block grant funds and convinced Tyler banks to commit more than $25 million through a lender commitment program to finance promising opportunities in this area. This does not mean that Tyler banks are expected to operate under a different set of regulatory constraints than anybody else. It means that for economically significant loan opportunities, such as a local medical instrumentation company wishing to expand, Tyler bankers will go the extra mile—taking the time, if necessary, to tap expertise through the Health Science Center networks, through the Tyler Economic Development Council—wherever they need to go to evaluate the opportunity. The Tyler Economic Development Council will also help the bank look into any appropriate state and federal programs (typically underused in Texas). If the company needs additional equity to qualify for bank financing, Tyler will work with all parties to draw from the seed capital fund or other sources of funding to make the financing a sound deal.

The third community model results when an area already has a heavy concentration of industry dependent on a particular technology. An industry group concludes that the community has sufficient expertise in that one industry to justify targeted efforts to build on that base. The city of Richardson, for example, is pursing telecommunications investments that will build on the already vast local telecommunications industry base. The North Dallas Chamber of Commerce has identified advanced electronic imaging as another area of significant opportunity, based on the level of investment already in Dallas and the growth potential of that market. The efforts of these two communities are very new; they are now exploring what resources are available to them, whether bankers and investors will participate, what the universities can add to this effort, how to capitalize on what they already have to create success for North Dallas and the Metroplex.

Commitment, Community and Capital: Common Elements of Success

These three models draw in various ways on university capabilities, local financial resources and concentrations of industrial expertise. While quite different in structure, they have three common elements. The first key element very simply is commitment. The community leader or leaders stepped forward and assumed responsibility for the furtherance of that community's goals. The commitment of key leaders is an absolute must, needed to give the programs credibility, to bring the right players to the table and to add continuity.

The second element common to all three programs is full participation from the community in identifying resources and setting the target. Community leaders evaluated the unique strengths of the community, the sources of expertise, the sources of capital, the ability to secure *pro bono* assistance or space or technical facilities and then set a discrete, focused target—medical instrumentation, imaging, promising incubator tenants. They set one target. None of these communities is trying to solve the nation's competitiveness problem. That is not their concern. They just found that the economic competitiveness of their hometown, their area, their industrial sector could be enhanced significantly simply by focusing all the key elements of the community to work together toward a single goal.

The third essential element is capital—the bottom line and obviously the most tangible demonstration of any commitment. Where does capital come from in Texas in 1990 for small business and community efforts?

In some cases, capital is still coming from the banks. Banks now tell us that they have plenty of money to lend, but they have upped the ante on what is required to get it. Often, these model programs are simply helping businesses cope with the new, more demanding lending information requirements. In other cases, the community is asking its lenders, investors and bankers to commit to exerting an extra level of effort when considering projects that will forward the community's economic development target. The community then facilitates the investment by providing assistance, incentives and even equity. The Community Reinvestment Act is lending additional weight on the side of banks considering these kinds of projects a little more carefully.

Creative support and cooperation with the traditional lending institutions is one way to get capital into these projects. Others sources of capital include the Texas Capital Network, which is a computer-based network matching private investors with entrepreneurs. It is small, but it is growing fast. Another source of capital available to smaller Texas communities is the half-cent sales tax for economic development recently authorized by the Texas Legislature. I have mentioned that Tyler tapped their local industrial foundation, and they used their community development block grant program. Some communities, particularly in other states, have had strong participation from locally based pension funds. After all, why shouldn't the pension funds help build value into the community that is building the fund?

In summary, technological competitiveness is critical to our being full participants in the global economy of the 1990s. Our nation must address serious macroeconomic barriers if we are to succeed. But there are communities in Texas and around the nation that have come up with creative ways to address competitiveness barriers that are not dependent on changing macroeconomic policy, that are not dependent on federal solutions and that are not dependent on the state Capitol. They are doing it through the commitment of top community leaders, cooperation of a broad section of the community and creatively but carefully applied capital. They have identified community strengths and wrapped the resources around those strengths to achieve some clearly defined goals.

I would like to close with a parable from World War II, another time of great social and economic change. A man entered a restaurant and ordered a cup of coffee. During World War II, they would give you this little scrap of sugar. The man called over to the waitress and asked for more sugar, whereupon she cast a baleful eye on him and pronounced, "Stir what you have." Do not wait for Washington to solve the challenges of technological competitiveness and their impact on your community. Do not let the federal government set all the limits on what you can do, and do not wait on Austin. Set your target, focus your resources, and stir what you have.

The Third Deficit: The Shortfall in Public Investment

Edward M. Gramlich

I am supposed to be an expert on the infrastructure problem called *the third deficit.* I suppose everybody recognizes that the first two deficits are the budget deficit and the trade deficit. The third deficit came a few years ago in a political ad that was signed by several fairly liberal economists, arguing that just because we had these other deficits that we should not scrimp on our public investment. So they coined the phrase *the third deficit,* which is what I am discussing today.

Four facts have given currency to the phrase *the third deficit.* The first fact is that if you just look at the numbers and look at how much the country is investing in public capital, or public infrastructure as it is known, from 1958 to 1972 the growth in public capital stock was 2.5 percent a year, which was roughly the growth of real gross national product (GNP) for that period. This is *real* growth. From 1972 to 1978, there was some slackening in that growth rate. From 1978 on, growth barely has been positive. There essentially has been no change in the public capital stock for 12 years now, but there obviously has been growth in GNP. That is the first fact that people mention when they talk about the third deficit.

The second fact is that several economists, actually most of this work has come from the Federal Reserve System—David Aschauer, who writes out of the Federal Reserve Bank of Chicago, and Alicia Munnell, who writes out of the Federal Reserve Bank of Boston—have run regressions and noted very large productivity changes. It turns out that the public capital stock maps pretty well the productivity residual, so you can see that productivity drops at the same time that public capital stock drops. You run the regression, and you get notions of enormous productivity gains if we would add more public capital.

The third fact is that some people have done some rate-of-return studies. There are lots of these, and I will not list them all for you. You expectedly get a very large rate of return.

The fourth fact is that there are lots of casual, more ad hoc, but still real estimates of congestion delay and this kind of thing. The administration recently had a report on the transportation system. They tallied up several billion dollars just in delay costs waiting for planes, waiting in rush hour traffic, and so forth. So you get a lot of estimates of a big shortfall in public capital and that this is really holding back the country.

The First Order of Business: Get the Price Structure Right

I am one of your delegates from the Northeast part of the country, that hotbed of liberals. You probably think that I am going to say, "Well, we should throw billions of dollars at this infrastructure problem and get things straightened out." Frankly, I am not going to say that. First, we do not actually have billions of dollars to throw around that readily. We all know that in the national government we have a very large deficit, or shortfall of national saving, which I think is a more meaningful way to put it. Lots of states have their own budget deficit problems. My own state of Michigan has quite a serious one that has been largely swept under the rug due to the exigencies of a political campaign. There really is a big problem in just paying for what we have now, let alone for what we do not have. Second, the tax wishes are certainly very clear. People do not necessarily want to pay a lot of taxes.

So my message will not be that we should throw billions of dollars at the third deficit, the infrastructure problem. My message will be, on the other hand, that a lot of what is holding us back is that we do not have the price structure right, and that we really should get that right before we start talking about third deficits. If we do that, a lot of the problems may solve themselves. It will not necessarily be easy to get the price structure right, but that is the main theme. The main theme is not just throwing money at the third deficit; the main theme is to try to get the price structure right.

This will mean a fairly simple answer to the questions, What is the third deficit, and what should we do about it? The answer is user fees. We could make much better use of user fees on a wide range of public capital of which we are short. This solves several economic and political problems, among which it may cut down the estimate of exactly what the third deficit is. We have heard Alan Greenspan's eloquent testimony to the virtues of a market economy, so I cannot begin to do justice to that, but let me mention a few points about the user-fee approach to infrastructure investment coming from the perspective of a basically market-oriented economist.

First, user fees provide an automatic source of revenue for the investment. Second, given the requirement that the user fees finance the structure, there is an automatic indication of when you have enough or when you do not have enough. If you assess a user fee and there is still excess demand, then you must raise the price. If there is excess supply, you can lower the price or user fee. This kind of simple market logic will work in a wide variety of places. There is an automatic indication of when you have too much or too little capital. Third, the user-fee approach has the economic and political value that those who benefit from the structure are those who pay. Fourth, this solves something that in the jargon of economics is known as the *externality problem.* If you have users from outside the community, which is a typical problem with public-sector capital, assessing a user fee can solve that problem, too. You can get those out-of-the-community users automatically to pay as well.

I turn to politics with great humility because no economist understands politics very well. I do not think many political scientists understand politics very well, and perhaps many politicians do not understand politics very well. But one thing that seems abundantly clear in today's world is that nobody likes to pay taxes if they do not see pretty clearly where those taxes are going. If there is one way to read all the election results and the political posturing and so forth of the 1980s, it seems to be that this is something that everybody must keep well in mind.

The second proposition is a little less clear to me, and that is, supposing people realize where their money is going and are reasonably sure that when they pay a user fee that the fee would in some way come back in the form of higher services from the public capital stock, would they then be willing to pay? I do not want to make any great claims there; I do not know if they would then be willing to pay or not. We have a lot of local referenda in Ann Arbor, Michigan, on these matters, and sometimes they pass, sometimes they do not pass. It is pretty hard to read clear teachings into that. But I guess that given the political realities as they are, I would rather try a user-fee approach than a blanket-tax approach. It seems to me that the user fee may not solve all the political problems, but it comes out a lot better than just paying taxes.

There is one drawback of user fees, which is that if income distribution is an important part of the issue, then the user-fee approach will not work. I will come back to that issue at the end of my talk, but I would rather accentuate the positive and talk about the variety of cases in which the user fee will work.

In the paper of which this talk is a short summary, I discuss a variety of types of public capital in which there is an alleged shortfall problem, and I basically talk about how the user-fee strategy would work in each of those cases. Let me quickly go down the list so you can get the flavor of what some of these types are. The first case is one in which you have local capital without a lot of spillovers from community to community; that is, basically the local people would buy the capital and use it, and there are not a lot of effects on people outside the jurisdiction. In the Northeast and Northcentral states, the outstanding example of this is the landfill problem. I do not know to what extent that is a problem in the Southwest. When flying in, I was struck by the fact that the land density is much different than it is on my side of the country. But I think it probably will be a problem here at some point, if it is not already. It strikes me that the landfill problem, at least in the Northeast, is characterized by the fact that there is basically nowhere to bury garbage anymore. The further problem is that homeowners have been viewing free garbage pickup as an entitlement for all these many years. We have provided this free service, and we have buried this stuff. Now the landfills are full, there is nowhere to put it, and nobody knows what to do.

Maybe if I talk about this in Texas you can head off the problem before it hits here, but basically the problem is that burying garbage and trash pickup in general is not an entitlement. It is costly. Land is costly, and there is not infinite space in which to bury stuff. We should make people pay for using this. If a service is free, we will overuse it just like in the Northeast. So the obvious solution to the landfill problem is to have households pay for disposal by the bag or something on that order. We have had a local proposal to do that in Ann Arbor. There is intense debate about this. The proposal in Ann Arbor is for a $1 per bag of garbage after the first, which strikes me as fine because my kids are in college now, my wife works hard, we are hardly ever home, and we never get to more than one bag a week. I think it is a wonderful proposal. But I would even be willing to pay for the first bag just because I am an economist, and economists are funny that way.

Anyway, not everyone has the religion, so this proposal has been met with intense opposition from those who feel free garbage pickup is an entitlement. That seems to be their view. It is crazy. People can look at the landfill; they recognize that it is full. They recognize that there are houses or something nice everywhere else. There is no other place to put garbage. If we get other communities to take the garbage, it is very costly because they do not want it either. So we seem to be on a treadmill to nowhere. I guess the lesson is that these services should be charged and that you are better off doing it sooner than later because if you get to it later, then landfill space is very expensive and then this fee is so high that you can encourage a lot of cheating—that is, basically you dump the garbage in someone else's yard or something like that.

The next type of capital is what I will call *local projects with spillovers.* By that I mean things such as highway systems—the interstate highway program is a good example—or airports, things of that nature in which the capital is in a community and it mainly benefits those in that community, but it also benefits outsiders, too. Again, I think the user-fee approach is the ideal way to solve this problem.

Why Federal Grants Have Been Hamstringing the Country

Until now, the country has been hamstrung, and one reason we have these third deficit estimates is that we have had a very perverse financing structure for these types of capital equipment. The structure basically is that these things are financed by grants from the federal government; grants have the property that there is very generous matching—80 percent or 90 percent—for a limited amount of money, and then no more money. So the locality is looking at a price structure that building a facility of a certain size is almost free, and then you take this enormous jump in the price and you have to pay full cost. So everybody exhausts their free funds, underbuilds the facility, there is congestion, and it is all the federal government's fault.

The price of getting the federal grant is that the local community or the state cannot use user fees. So if you get interstate highway money, in general you cannot put up toll gates. Or if you get airport grant money, you cannot charge a fee to use the airport.

The obvious solution—my solution—to that would be to get rid of the federal grants. Let the community put up a toll gate or airport fee, and outsiders using that facility will pay the fee like anybody else. You have an automatic solution to this problem. We have been gradually moving in that direction in recent years. I think 10 states are permitted to put up toll gates on interstate highways as an experiment. States have always been permitted to put up toll gates on bridges, but now it is expanded to an experimental program.

The recent budget bill contains some fine print that probably most people do not know about, but I think it is very important in this regard. There is now a provision that if an airport wants to, it can charge a user fee for using the airport. This could raise the price of a flight by $12 maximum for a plane traveler; it is $3 per arrival and departure from an airport. This fee would give some airports a lot more money than they would ever get from a federal grant. If the airports do this, they cannot take the federal grant. I think this is a welcome change, and I expect that this will do a lot to solve the airport congestion problem. It may not solve all of it, because $3 per flight may not be enough; I do not know why they put that limit, but they did. That is politics. I will certainly congratulate Congress on a long-overdue change, one that moves in the right direction.

Another aspect in this vein is higher education—my own industry. Again, the approach until now for state universities has been pretty much to send delegations to the state Capitol with a tin cup. If the Legislature does not want to fill the tin cup, then universities can charge tuition. State universities are a pretty good buy in this country. People want to come, and if we have to charge tuition—especially to out-of-state students, but even to in-state students—what is wrong with that? I do not see anything wrong with that. There is an income-distribution problem that I mentioned earlier, but there are also scholarship sources and student loans and so forth, so I think we can deal with that. But the idea is that basically we have a lot of users of these facilities that should be paying full shot.

Now I get to the exceptions. There are a couple of cases in which my logic does not work perfectly. There are some types of facilities in which user fees physically cannot be assessed. Waste-water treatment is one example, and there may be some others. There are not many exceptions if you actually look at those types of public capital in which we are in deficit, and for those—what do you do? Well, I would continue the federal grant for now but with a crucial change. Rather than making the matching rate 90 percent–10 percent for a small amount of capital and then you have to pay full price, I would like to try to estimate on the typical federal grant the balance of internal and external users. For example, one-third of the users of a facility are from out of state or out of the jurisdiction, then the matching rate on the federal grant should be 30 percent federal, not 90 percent. Just switching grants to that system would make a big difference in the economic incentives on the facility.

There is also a trust fund problem. A lot of facilities are financed by a trust fund; again, airports are a primary example. The ticket tax goes into a trust fund, but the trust fund—because of some political magic—does not pay all the costs of the facility. In the case of airports, the trust fund pays for the capital expansion but not for the traffic controllers. Again, there is a general revenue subsidy to the facility that I think is pointless. If you go the user-fee route, I think you also want to clean the trust fund side.

Finally, nothing that I say here works about public education. There is one outstanding example of where the user-fee approach will not work—local public education. Our democracy is all about income mixing in the public schools. Public schools are free; that is a basic part of America. I think it is a part that we all hold quite dear. I do not want anything that I say to extend to public education. I think we are stuck with the same old power equalization problems that we have always had.

However, the fact that the user fee, or really the benefit-payer approach, does not work on every type of public capital that we need should not close our mind to the value of this approach. If we apply this approach across the board, I think that a lot of this talk about the third deficit would go away, in part because we would have more money to finance some structures and in part because we might see on an economic basis that we really may not need all this capital. There would be an automatic way to regulate supply and demand of the structure.

Financing the Future: Private and Public Funding

Dan W. Cook, III

I will divide this discussion into two parts. First, how will we fund our businesses in the 1990s? Second, how will we fund the environment, namely the state of Texas, in which we hope our businesses will flourish in the 1990s and beyond?

I think I can dispatch financing our businesses rather quickly because I do not know the answer, and I am in a business that spends a lot of time giving thought to this. Fortunately, we are financing day to day, and our crystal ball does not have to be very good. We tap whichever markets are available at the time.

Let me talk about some traditional sources, traditional markets, on which we have relied heavily over the years that seem to be unavailable to us today. Traditional sources, such as commercial banks, insurance companies and equity markets, have certain problems. I will make some generalizations, and there certainly are exceptions to these. I do not think there are very many exceptions, unfortunately.

Banks on the Defensive

Let's start with banks. Banks are on the defensive, and in my opinion they are in disarray. They have more assets—poor assets—than they would like to have, many are severely capital short, and they have little access to capital markets. Equity markets are making an assessment of what the banks are doing. Currently, money center banks are selling at 50 percent of book value, all except a couple. Some banks are selling as low as 20 percent. Regional banks are also selling at a discount to book value; they are selling at 75 percent, on average. The market is very selective on the regional banks. Overcapacity in the industry and limited access to capital, in my opinion, will accelerate the rapid pace of consolidation of the financial services sector. Some very knowledgeable officials at the Office of Thrift Supervision told me that they predict by the year 2000 there may be as few as 50 lending institutions in this country. That number is down from some 14,500 not too many years ago. I do not know if that is an accurate or valid projection, but I think it is probably something that may be very much necessary to beat on a global basis. Some of the other participants today talked about how we should be able to lead ourselves to fight on a global basis. Certainly our competition abroad does not have as fractured a system as we have here in the United States.

People in this room may quibble with this statement, but I maintain that banks today are not lending to business. In Texas, that statement is particularly true. All except one bank appear to have shut their lending window. I do not worry about the ads that are being run. If you want a loan, go ask for it, and then find out if they are making the loans. All the largest, most credit-worthy companies can borrow, and they have access to the commercial paper market. A recent survey done by my firm—Goldman, Sachs—of *Fortune* 1,000 chief financial officers in industrial and service companies confirms that there is indeed a credit crunch despite opinions to the contrary.

Let me give you a startling fact. In the early 1970s, banks and thrift companies accounted for 80 percent of the credit market lending in this country. In the past two years, less than 20 percent of the credit lending in this country was provided by banks and thrift companies. Institutions that are supposed to be providing capital credit to the market are providing less than 20 percent. If you look at the slope, it looks like the south face of Zermatt. The Japanese banks now have discovered that they have some problems. They have had some bad real estate loans, and they dipped their toe a little in situations in which they should not have been. Their capital adequacy also is being stretched, and we, like other investment bankers, are being asked to address that.

Insurance companies have substantial weaknesses on the asset side stemming from leverage transactions in real estate. Real estate development loans on a nonrecourse basis are virtually nonexistent. Recently, Equitable Life just walked away from an investment in a recourse deal in Manhattan. When major insurance companies start doing this, you have to ask, "What is the future for real estate?"

I guess this leaves us with the equity market as the primary funding source. When one encounters the re-equitization of U.S. business following a decade of restructuring and leverage, the real question is, Can the equity markets cover the expansion, fuel the expansion, after all its debts are repaid? I do not know the answer, but I expect the equity markets will become very selective and will present a very real challenge to corporate financial officers.

Funding for Texas in the 1990s

Let me now shift to another area for funding in the 1990s, which is important to any business person in the state; that is, How will Texas finance itself in the 1990s, given a wide array of problems? These problems include educational problems, court system problems, workers compensation, criminal justice and mental health, just to name the most obvious. Let me give you some idea of the magnitude of the financing problem and the options for funding as I see them.

I served on the Texas Select Committee on Tax Equity, which was formed a couple of years ago. The committee was composed of 13 members, one of whom got the job by acclamation—and that was Bob Bullock, who was then comptroller of accounts. There were 12 other members, four picked by each of the three senior officers in the state—four picked by the governor, four by the lieutenant governor and four by the speaker of the House. More than 50 percent of the committee members were businessmen, and I thought they were pretty good businessmen. The rest of the committee members were from the Senate and the House. This committee met for about 18 months, and we went to 12 different cities. We tried to be good listeners to determine what tax policy could be and should be. We adopted a mission statement, which said, "The mission of the Select Committee on Tax Equity is to recommend to the state the standards and options for developing a fair, viable and economically competitive state and local tax system capable of generating sufficient revenues to meet the expected needs of the future." We did not quite accomplish that mission because all our efforts were concentrated on a revenue-neutral procedure. That was what we tried to target. We tried to examine where the fairness was and where it was not, and we wanted to make sure that we did not take an archaic, patchwork-quilt operation into the 1990s. We heard some 400 hours of testimony. In January 1989, we rendered a final report, published as *Rethinking Texas Taxes.* We made several conclusions, but I will not discuss those right now. Virtually nothing was done; none of our suggestions was adopted.

But I am encouraged because I think that for the first time we will really see quite a focus in this next Legislature, which convenes in January. One of the people who basically hired the people here—Gib Lewis—is still speaker of the House. One of the fellows who I think is probably the most knowledgeable man in Texas—Bob Bullock—is now lieutenant governor, presiding over the Senate. We have a lady who appeared before the committee and who made a very fine presentation and understands a lot about tax rules in Texas—Ann Richards—who will become governor next year. We also have someone who will be a speaker tomorrow afternoon—Dan Morales—who was a very valuable member

Table 1
Key Problems with the Current System

- It does not grow with the economy or the demand for services. This makes periodic tax bills inevitable.
- It is not fair. It falls most heavily on poor and middle-income Texans.
- Among businesses, its burden falls on a handful of industries—many escape state and local taxes almost entirely.
- Although the overall burden is low, major taxes fall on capital investment and may hurt competitiveness.
- It is becoming increasingly unbalanced among sources, and rates of the major taxes are approaching possible ceilings, leading into inflexibility at the local level.
- Inability (or unwillingness) to address fiscal problems comprehensively promotes uncertainty.

Source: *Rethinking Texas Taxes*, pp. 29–34.

of the committee and who will be the attorney general starting next year. So, I am encouraged.

Understanding the Tax Structure in Texas

Let's talk very quickly about our current system and its structure (*Table 1*). Texas relies very heavily on sales taxes at the state level and on property taxes at the local level. No one seems to like property taxes, but people tend not to be too concerned about sales taxes—I guess because we pay our sales taxes piecemeal, and it does not seem to hurt as much. With property tax, we write one check a year, and it hurts like heck. Nearly 70 percent of the state's tax revenues come from those two taxes, whereas somewhere near 50 percent of U.S. taxes come from those same sources (*Chart 1*).

Of the total revenues raised in the state, $12 billion comes from tax collection (*Chart 2*). Of that $12 billion, 50 percent comes from sales tax (*Chart 3*). When you look at motor fuels, motor vehicles, etc., Texas is somewhere around 70 percent total taxes on consumption. This is very, very high compared with everywhere else.

Chart 1
Texas and U.S. State and Local Tax Mix, 1987

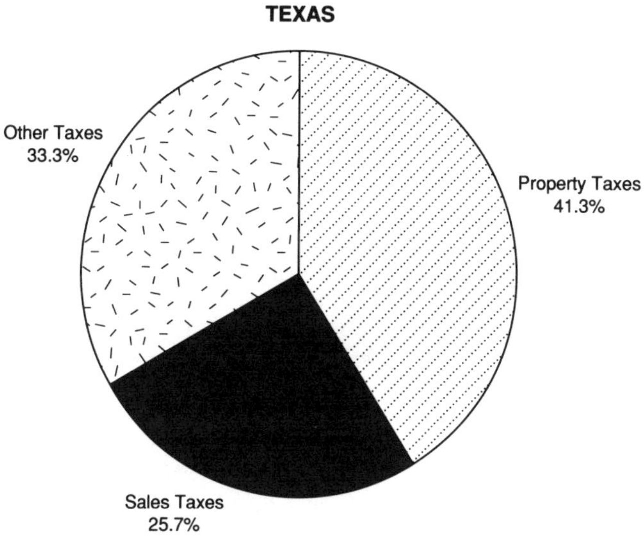

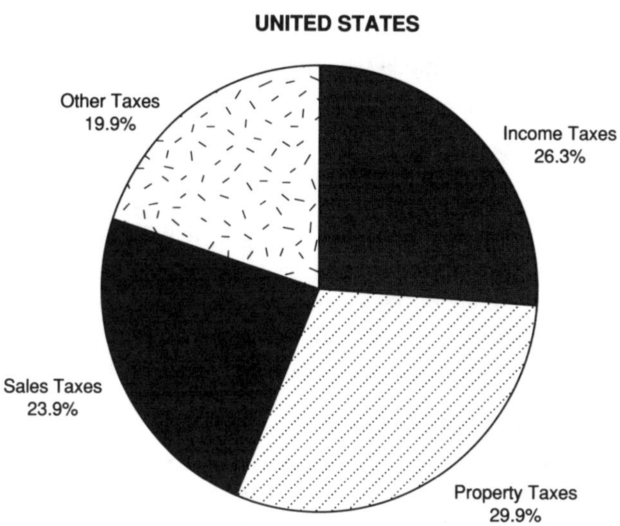

Source: U.S. Department of Commerce, Bureau of the Census, *Government Finances in 1986–87* (Washington, D.C., November 1988), as reprinted in *Rethinking Texas Taxes*, p. 10.

Chart 2
Texas State Revenue by Source, 1988

(Millions of dollars)

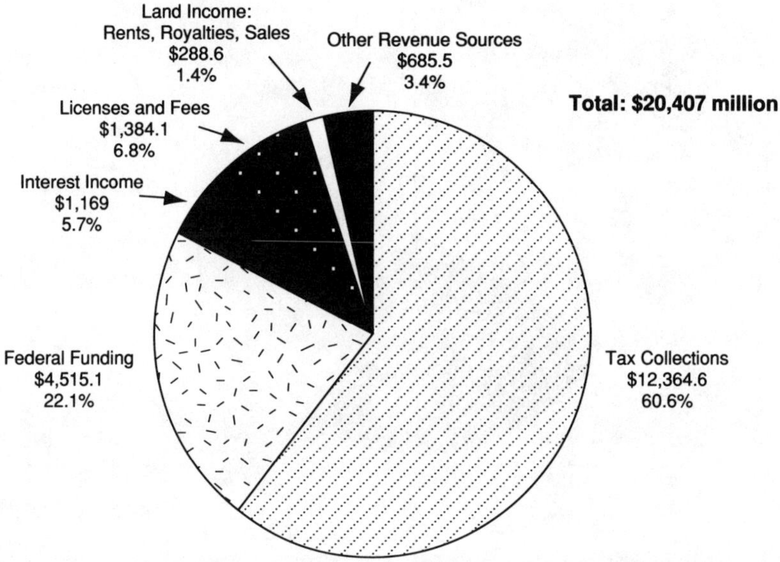

Source: Comptroller of Public Accounts, *Annual Financial Report*, 1988, as reprinted in *Rethinking Texas Taxes*, p. 11.

One of the ways to measure this is to look at the state revenues as a percentage of per capita income (*Table 2*). How do we stack up against other states? Over the past eight years, Texas' growth of revenues as a percentage of per capita income actually was well below the U.S. average. In tax burden rankings on a per capita basis, Texas ranks 30th overall (*Table 3*). In terms of gross state product, Texas ranks 48th. Texas ranks 31st in state and local government spending per capita (*Table 4*).

What is our capacity, and how much do we avail ourselves of it? On an index of 100, Texas is ranked at 111 (*Table 5*). We have excess capacity above 100 to tax. Texas is ranked at 81 for the amount of tax effort made, so the difference between the two is 30. We have a lot of capacity to tax, but we underutilize it. I am not saying that is a negative; it is probably a positive.

Chart 3
Texas State Tax Revenue, 1988

(Millions of dollars)

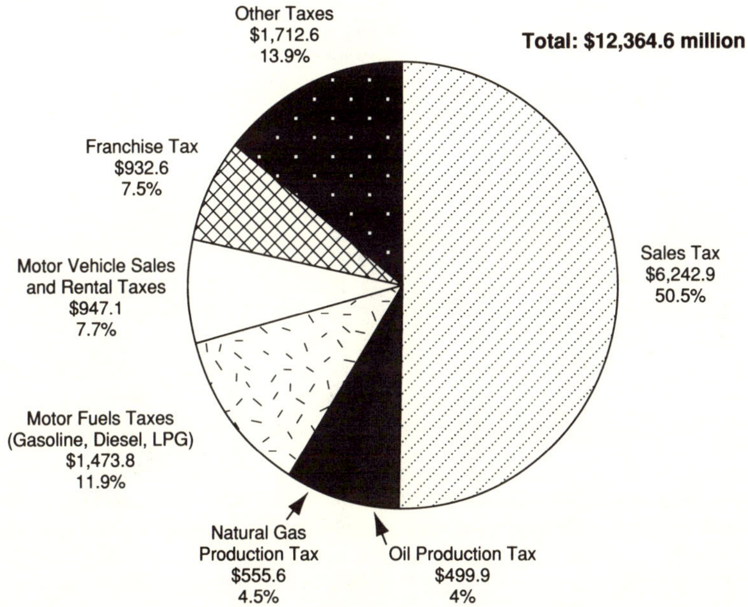

Source: Comptroller of Public Accounts, *Annual Financial Report*, 1988, as reprinted in *Rethinking Texas Taxes*, p. 11.

Table 2
State Revenues as a Percent of State Per Capita Income

	1981	1988	Change as percent
Texas	12.3	4.9	+21
U.S. Average	13.4	15.0	+12

Source: The Tax Foundation.

Table 3
Tax Burden Rankings, 1986

	Dollars Per Capita	Rank	Percent of Personal Income	Rank	Percent of Gross State Product	Rank
Alabama	1,022	48	9.01	46	7.53	46
Alaska	4,489	1	25.24	1	12.25	2
Arizona	1,476	20	10.95	15	9.20	20
Arkansas	1,011	49	9.13	44	7.58	44
California	1,727	10	10.21	26	8.73	24
Colorado	1,485	18	9.75	36	8.20	31
Connecticut	1,947	4	9.94	31	11.34	4
Delaware	1,661	13	11.07	13	8.98	22
Florida	1,273	35	8.70	48	8.37	29
Georgia	1,280	34	9.52	40	7.59	43
Hawaii	1,785	7	11.99	5	9.81	9
Idaho	1,054	47	9.39	42	8.02	35
Illinois	1,546	16	9.92	33	8.52	27
Indiana	1,227	38	9.34	43	7.95	37
Iowa	1,417	23	10.62	19	9.22	18
Kansas	1,394	27	9.52	41	8.08	33
Kentucky	1,103	45	9.82	35	7.74	40
Louisiana	1,253	36	11.20	11	7.58	45
Maine	1,414	24	11.06	14	9.58	12
Maryland	1,742	8	10.33	23	10.16	7
Massachusetts	1,933	5	10.91	16	9.76	10
Michigan	1,703	12	11.53	8	10.17	6
Minnesota	1,715	11	11.44	10	9.56	13
Mississippi	965	50	9.93	32	7.96	36
Missouri	1,152	42	8.35	49	6.99	49
Montana	1,376	28	11.66	7	9.26	17
Nebraska	1,338	29	9.74	37	8.06	34
Nevada	1,559	15	10.09	28	7.73	41
New Hampshire	1,216	40	7.64	50	6.74	50
New Jersey	1,868	6	10.03	30	9.20	19
New Mexico	1,241	37	10.87	17	7.78	39
New York	2,539	3	14.84	3	12.44	1
North Carolina	1,222	39	9.82	34	7.66	42
North Dakota	1,284	32	10.30	24	8.13	32
Ohio	1,412	25	10.13	27	8.62	25
Oklahoma	1,284	33	10.45	22	8.52	28

(continued)

Table 3—*continued*
Tax Burden Rankings, 1986

	Dollars Per Capita	Rank	Percent of Personal Income	Rank	Percent of Gross State Product	Rank
Oregon	1,436	22	10.77	18	9.39	15
Pennsylvania	1,459	21	10.24	25	9.45	14
Rhode Island	1,532	17	10.51	21	9.82	8
South Carolina	1,138	44	10.07	29	8.59	26
South Dakota	1,142	43	9.66	38	8.24	30
Tennessee	1,077	46	8.97	47	7.15	47
TEXAS	**1,292**	**30**	**9.58**	**39**	**7.10**	**48**
Utah	1,292	31	11.76	6	8.96	23
Vermont	1,484	19	11.12	12	9.30	16
Virginia	1,404	26	9.11	45	7.80	38
Washington	1,589	14	10.59	20	9.13	21
West Virginia	1,214	41	11.48	9	9.67	11
Wisconsin	1,730	9	12.44	4	10.76	5
Wyoming	2,628	2	20.55	2	11.41	3

Source: U.S. Department of Commerce, Bureau of the Census, *Government Finances in 1985–86*; Bureau of Economic Analysis, *Survey of Current Business, May 1988.*

Smoke, Mirrors and the $2.5-Billion Budget Gap

Let's talk about the problem going forward. I will give a primer on some of the funding sources. Let's look at the state budget for a moment. The good news is the Legislative Budget Board base budget of reference is only $32 billion; the bad news is that they raised it about $700 million a few weeks ago. But let's just use this number for reference. If you add to it the various items that must be added to restore it—say we robbed some things and now we will make it whole again—we come up with about $34 billion in total appropriations. This is for 1992–93. If you add to it some additional revenues, just for growth, etc., you come up with $31 billion. There is a funding gap of $2.5 billion when you subtract those figures (*Table 6*).

Everyone says, "Well, what the heck is $2.5 billion? We have suffered before, and we found ways to raid other places. We have smoke and mirrors." I maintain that our new lieutenant governor, Bob Bullock, knows more about smoke and mirrors than anyone else in the state. He knows the smoke and mirrors largely

Table 4
State and Local Government Spending Per Capita, 1987

State	Per Capita Government Spending	Rank	State Share of Total (Percent)
Alaska	$11,281	1	74.6
Wyoming	4,951	2	67.2
New York*	4,683	3	56.9
Washington	3,802	4	57.9
Minnesota	3,758	5	57.7
California*	3,745	6	60.3
Massachusetts	3,602	7	66.5
Colorado	3,449	8	48.0
New Jersey*	3,431	9	65.2
Nebraska	3,431	10	41.7
Arizona	3,385	11	51.5
Utah	3,357	12	57.8
Michigan*	3,333	13	61.3
Nevada	3,288	14	60.7
Delaware	3,287	15	73.3
Oregon	3,281	16	57.5
Montana	3,250	17	64.6
Connecticut	3,237	18	64.1
Hawaii	3,191	19	75.6
North Dakota	3,170	20	74.4
Wisconsin	3,154	21	62.2
Rhode Island	3,113	22	73.6
Maryland	3,084	23	62.3
Vermont	3,065	24	68.7
New Mexico	2,988	25	73.8
Ohio*	2,922	26	65.9
Louisiana	2,912	27	65.1
Georgia	2,892	28	50.4
Illinois*	2,885	29	56.3
Tennessee	2,859	30	47.4
TEXAS*	**2,816**	**31**	**45.9**
Kansas	2,814	32	52.1
Iowa	2,814	33	63.6
Pennsylvania*	2,792	34	61.7
Florida*	2,749	35	46.7
South Dakota	2,744	36	65.9

(continued)

Table 4—*continued*
State and Local Government Spending Per Capita, 1987

State	Per Capita Government Spending	Rank	State Share of Total (Percent)
Maine	2,737	37	70.4
Virginia	2,641	38	62.2
West Virginia	2,635	39	76.8
Oklahoma	2,628	40	64.1
North Carolina*	2,624	41	60.2
South Carolina	2,556	42	68.1
New Hampshire	2,476	43	56.7
Alabama	2,475	44	62.7
Indiana	2,425	45	62.2
Kentucky	2,383	46	71.3
Idaho	2,361	47	68.1
Missouri	2,329	48	59.8
Mississippi	2,306	49	65.4
Arkansas	2,185	50	66.6
U.S. Average	**3,185**	—	**58.8**

* One of the 10 most populous states, according to current Census Bureau estimates.
Source: U.S. Department of Commerce, Bureau of the Census, *Government Finances in 1986–87* (November 1988), as reprinted in *Rethinking Texas Taxes*, p. 21.

have been used up. We do not have much room if you take the $2.5 billion gap and make some pretty conservative additions here to make up for school problems we have, such as the *Edgewood vs. Kirby* decision. Of course, we realize that we added $500 million last session, but we were told it was unconstitutional. So, we do not know how high it will go. To summarize, when you add everything, you can come up with numbers ranging between $2.8 billion and $5.3 billion. But where does it come from? Let's go back and look at the sources and some of the myths that people have about how we can solve this problem.

The following are some of the myths about solving the public finance problem:

- *If we wanted to, we could solve all our problems simply by cutting the budget.* I think there is obviously fat in the budget. There is waste in Austin, but I was convinced after spending some time there that they have

Table 5
Representative Tax System Indexes of State and Local Tax Capacity and Effort, 1986

	Tax Capacity	Rank	Tax Effort	Rank
Alabama	75	48	103	15
Alaska	259	1	121	4
Arizona	99	20	95	33
Arkansas	74	49	91	39
California	120	6	94	34
Colorado	118	7	88	45
Connecticut	127	4	89	42
Delaware	123	5	96	30
Florida	103	15	85	46
Georgia	90	33	100	18
Hawaii	117	8	98	27
Idaho	78	45	94	35
Illinois	96	26	97	29
Indiana	87	38	98	25
Iowa	84	40	112	6
Kansas	99	22	96	32
Kentucky	78	44	90	41
Louisiana	97	25	98	24
Maine	89	35	98	26
Maryland	104	14	99	20
Massachusetts	113	10	97	28
Michigan	94	28	117	5
Minnesota	101	17	122	3
Mississippi	69	50	106	11
Missouri	90	31	83	47
Montana	90	32	105	14
Nebraska	94	29	99	21
Nevada	146	3	78	49
New Hampshire	112	11	66	50
New Jersey	117	9	96	31
New Mexico	99	21	92	38
New York	101	19	144	1
North Carolina	86	39	92	37
North Dakota	102	16	106	10
Ohio	91	30	100	17
Oklahoma	105	13	91	40

(continued)

Table 5—*continued*
Representative Tax System Indexes of State and Local Tax Capacity and Effort, 1986

	Tax Capacity	Rank	Tax Effort	Rank
Oregon	95	27	106	13
Pennsylvania	89	34	99	22
Rhode Island	88	37	108	9
South Carolina	77	47	102	16
South Dakota	82	42	89	43
Tennessee	83	41	89	44
TEXAS	**111**	**12**	**81**	**48**
Utah	81	43	110	8
Vermont	97	24	99	23
Virginia	98	23	92	36
Washington	101	18	100	19
West Virginia	77	46	106	12
Wisconsin	89	36	123	2
Wyoming	169	2	111	7

Note: Compares each state to the national average of 100; that is, the index numbers for Texas indicate a tax capacity 111 percent above the national average and a tax effort 19 percent below the national average.

Source: Advisory Commission of Intergovernmental Relations, *Measuring State Fiscal Capacity.*

done a marvelous job of spending our money. I am not sure it is the most efficient way to spend it, but I really do not think there is a lot of waste in it. If people know where to cut it, the people in Austin would like to know about it.

- *The economy will improve, and recent problems will disappear.* If you believe that, then you will believe a lot of things. Let's hope that happens, but what happens if it does not?
- *Higher oil prices will solve our problems.* That is nonsense. The federal government and others will find their way to that pocket before we can find a way to get to it.
- *If we need more money for state and local government, we can easily raise it by taxing more items under the sales tax.* It is very difficult to broaden the sales tax base and very much more difficult to enforce and collect it.

Table 6
The Funding Gap Problem for 1992–93
(as of November 1990)

Appropriations	**1992–93 (Millions of dollars)**
LBB Base of Reference Estimate of Spending (excluding S.B. 1 costs)	32,271.3
Add:	
Repay TRS Delay	190.5
School Finance Bill (S.B. 1, 6th C.S.)	1,606.9
Repay Other Spending Items Delayed (6th C.S.)	11.2
Total Appropriations	**$34,079.9**
Revenues	
Revenue Base	**$29,696.4***
Add:	
Estimated Effect of "Improved" Revenue Outlook	825.0
Continuing Effects of 6th C.S. Tax Bills (3)	1,046.0
Total Revenues	31,567.4
The Funding Gap—Base of Reference Version	**2,512.5**
Add:	
LBB Estimated Emergency Appropriations	
• DHS—Various Programs	340.7
• MH/MR—Court Compliance	13.8
• Department of Health—Various Programs	5.0
• Attorney General—Workers' Compensation	13.0
Total Emergency Items	372.5
Unresolved Issue—TRS Underfunding	350.0
LBB High-Priority Items	
1. General Issues	
• 5-Percent Employee Pay Raise	595.0
• Employee Health Insurance Premium Increase	215.0
• Other Issues	63.0
2. Education Agency	
• Tax Effort Response in Tier 2 of the FSP (estimated at two-thirds of maximum)	224.9

(continued)

Table 6—*continued*
The Funding Gap Problem for 1992–93 (as of November 1990)

Appropriations	**1992–93 (Millions of dollars)**
2. Education Agency—*continued*	
• Increased Textbook Costs	31.1
• Facilities Funding (upper end of range)	100.0
3. Department of Human Services (upper range est.)	576.0
4. Department of Criminal Justice—County Jails Suit	275.3
Total High-Priority Items	2,080.3
Revised Funding Gap:	
With Emergency Items	**2,885.0**
With Emergency Items and TRS	**3,235.0**
With Emergency Items, TRS and High-Priority Items	**5,315.3**

* No official revenue estimate for 1992–93 is currently available. This estimate expands the 1990–91 estimate by 10 percent.

Source: *Rethinking Texas Taxes.*

- *If we need more money for state and local government, we can easily raise it by imposing a lottery.* Ann Richards made a lot of this topic. We ducked the issue. Frankly, it was a hot potato, and we said that a lottery was not a tax, so we did not have to spend a lot of time on it. We did spend some time on it, and our conclusion was that at best we could count on $600 million a year. That is not hay, but it is certainly a long way from covering a $5 billion-plus gap, and that is just for the next two years. So, anyone who believes that the lottery is a panacea for our problems is kidding himself.

Let's talk about tax policy alternatives (*Table 7*). One is to increase the sales tax by 1 percent. That will create approximately $1.2 billion of annual revenues, and that is a very viable opportunity.

Today, Louisiana enjoys the distinction having the highest sales tax in the country (*Table 8*). The highest sales tax exists at the New Orleans airport; the rest of the state is not quite that high. I never thought I would see the day when our sales taxes were as high as New York's. This is the tax in Dallas. There are some 31 different sales taxes in Texas.

Table 7
Tax Policy Alternatives

	Annual Revenues (Billions of dollars)
Increase Sales Tax by 1 Percent	1.2
Expand Sales Tax	.8
Tax Insurance Premiums	1.2
Increase Motor Fuels Tax by 1 Cent Per Gallon	.1
Impose Corporate Income Tax or Value-Added Tax and Eliminate Franchise Tax	.5
Impose a Personal Income Tax of 2 Percent	3.7

Table 8
States with the Highest State and Local Sales Tax Rates

State	Rate (Percent)
Louisiana	10.00
Alabama	9.50
Illinois	9.25
Texas	8.25
New York	8.25

Table 9
How Texas and Other States Compare on Taxes

Per capita state taxes totaled $822.46 in 1989, 48th lowest.

The U.S. average per capita state tax total was $1,147.02, which is 39 percent higher than Texas' $822.46.

However, the state and local tax burden is higher; Texas ranks about 36th on that basis.

Comparing tax mixes between Texas and the United States,*

	Texas (percent)	U.S. average (percent)
Property tax	41.3	29.9
Sales tax	25.7	23.9
Income tax	0	26.3
Other taxes	33.0	19.9

Texas' sales tax rate, a combined 8.25 percent (state and local), ranks fourth highest in the nation.

Property-tax comparisons are harder, but the average effective tax rate on an existing single-family home in 1987 was $1.41 per $100, which is 13th highest.

* Source: U.S. Department of Commerce, Bureau of the Census, *Government Finances in 1986–87* (November 1988), as reprinted in *Rethinking Texas Taxes*, p. 17.

How much more can we raise the sales tax? Can we raise it 1 percent? Can we raise it 2 percent? For most of the people in this room that is not difficult to answer. Let's go ahead and do it. It will not change our spending a bit. The problem is that the sales tax is one of the most regressive taxes that you can possibly put on people, and it is only a delay until you have to do something else. Even if we could expand the sales tax to a wider range of other businesses, we pick up only $0.8 billion.

Taxing insurance premiums could bring $1.2 billion. I will drop that one like a hotcake. We are not about to do that. It was a wild dream by someone in a session in Austin at 11 p.m. when no one was watching the store, but fortunately we stopped that one.

Increasing the motor fuels tax by 1 cent per gallon would give us $0.1 billion—small change. Imposing a corporate income tax or a value-added tax and eliminating the franchise tax could bring $0.5 billion. If you do that, you will have a corporate income tax, and that is where it will stop. It will be antibusiness and against policy for maintaining business in the state. Imposing a personal income tax of 2 percent would generate $3.7 billion. That is no big surprise; everyone knows there is a lot of money with this option.

We have just discussed an analysis that shows that the gap is $5 billion. We see how we can raise it. The answer clearly is that we will have a state personal income tax. The question is, When will we have it? We can do it in a couple of ways. We can either let the people in Austin do it, or we can hope it goes away. We can use the remaining smoke and mirrors. We can probably avoid it this legislative session, but can we avoid it in the next session?

I really think that business should be proactive. I think business should take time to study and analyze the problem, and if the analysis is as I have suggested it is, I think we should explain to business the needs for taxation (*Table 9*). We should go to communities and tell them what is needed and why it is needed rather than let the elected officials do it, because elected officials are afraid of the electorate. They do not want to do that. They have to run for office next time. We should prepare the waters for them to do what is right, and we should do it now.

My feeling is that there is nobody in this room who would finance their business on an unprofessional basis. In this state, we have tiptoed through a minefield of political problems for many years. I really think that if we do not solve the financing problem, someone else will do it for us. To borrow a line from a popular London musical I saw recently—*Miss Saigon*—we are going to have a personal income tax and a corporate profits tax, conceived in hell and born in strife if we do not do it ourselves. So, let's be a part of it. According to the comptroller, it takes somewhere between two years and four years to have this system fully implementational. If we wait until 1994 or 1995 to address this problem and try to jam this thing, I am not sure how we will finance our debt.

PART FOUR

Perspectives on the Energy Market

"Despite substantial differences in supplies, demands and prices, there is an agreement across models and scenarios that the world economy will become increasingly more dependent on Persian Gulf oil over the next decade."

—Hillard G. Huntington

"We estimate that by the year 2000 at least 5,000 horizontal wells will be drilled, representing an annual growth rate of almost 20 percent. We are convinced that this will be the fastest-growing segment of domestic drilling."

—Isaac C. Kerridge, Jr.

"Without politics, the Middle East today would be producing 30 million barrels of oil."

—Edward N. Krapels

Oil: Alternative Perspectives on the Decade

Hillard G. Huntington

The dynamics of oil-price formation are similar to my cooking Indian food; my curry tastes different each time I make it. Sometimes, when one stirs the pot of oil-price curry, a strong taste of economics comes through. At other times, politics is the dominant flavor. And right now, the curry has the distinct flavor of psychology and military science.

Over time, I expect the economic flavor to come through more distinctly and force prices down from today's level. But these conditions may materialize only after some sharp turns in oil prices in response to developments in the Persian Gulf crisis. They may also take months to be realized.

Over the next several years, rivalry among members of OPEC may exacerbate this price decline as they try to put Humpty Dumpty together again. Who will reduce output to allow Iraq and Kuwait back into the club? Over the long run, it is difficult to know whether the Iraqi invasion of Kuwait has permanently altered the sustained price path for oil. This outcome will depend significantly on whether the monarchial states, such as Saudi Arabia, or the populist Arab states, such as Iraq, dominate in the post-invasion political scene. Does a continued U.S. military presence reduce the risk of oil investment in the region or increase the tension of a rising Arab populist mood against Western incursions into this politically volatile region? And what about the actions of major oil-consuming countries? Does a third shock in 18 years significantly increase their efforts to find alternatives to gasoline as a transportation fuel?

Acknowledgment

I have greatly benefited from the many ideas and insights of the EMF 11 Working Group members and the group's chairman, W. David Montgomery. I want to acknowledge their significant contributions, but I also emphasize that the conclusions in this article are mine and should not necessarily be attributed to the working group.

For all these reasons, I suspect that it will be difficult to discern for some time whether we have actually entered a new regime for oil markets. Any evaluation will have to deal with some basic economic factors that shape this market, and those are the issues that I would like to discuss.

The Energy Modeling Forum Study

My remarks focus on long-run oil market trends, not on short-run consequences of oil disruptions. My conclusions are based on results from an Energy Modeling Forum (EMF) comparison of model results focusing on international oil supplies and demands. EMF was founded in 1976 at Stanford University to help improve the use and usefulness of models for developing insights about energy markets and key energy issues. Each study is conducted through an ad hoc working group of some 40 decisionmakers and analysts from industry, government and academia. The current working group is chaired by W. David Montgomery, assistant director for commerce and natural resources, U.S. Congressional Budget Office. The analysis for our oil study was completed before the Iraqi invasion of Kuwait, so my remarks assume that oil prices will return to pre-invasion levels over the next year.

My major points include three key observations. First, after many years of changing energy prices, fluctuating economic growth and shifting government policies, there is little agreement about future oil supply and demand trends. Second, this range of views on supply and demand can lead to very different assessments of the long-run, sustained oil-price paths over the next decade or two. Decisionmakers should plan for a range of future prices. And third, despite these uncertainties, there is agreement on the increasing dependence on Persian Gulf oil across a range of models and scenarios. Furthermore, policy actions for limiting oil imports may be costly and difficult.

The working group analyzed 12 different scenarios, examining the oil markets under a range of different conditions. One scenario was based on the mid-price case in the Energy Information Administration's 1989 International Energy Outlook (IEO). After remaining relatively flat in the high teens through the early 1990s, the long-run, sustained oil-price path rises to $30 per barrel (in 1990 dollars) by 2000 and to $39 per barrel by 2010. This path shows the oil-price path that can be sustained over the long run; prices in the short run can be either above or below this path. Also, the possible effect of exchange rates on the dollar price of oil is not incorporated. The market economies are assumed to grow at 2.9 percent per annum over the 1988–2000 period in this scenario, called the *1989 IEO price case* in the study. Finally, any additional policies to reduce oil demand in the major economies are not incorporated. While one might expect some demand-reduction policies in the United States, other countries have already made considerable progress in shifting away from oil.

Alternative Perspectives on Oil Consumption

After leveling out during the 1980s, oil consumption in the market economies begins to rise in all models in this scenario, although at substantially different rates. Chart 1 highlights the projections of only three of the dozen models to demonstrate some key relationships. Demand grows modestly in the Energy Information Administration (EIA) and Canadian Energy Research Institute (CERI) projections but very strongly in the Harvard estimates. These estimates vary by as much as 15 million barrels per day in 1995 and by 30 million barrels per day in 2010. While disconcerting perhaps, this range should not be surprising. Analysts assign different values to demand responses to price, economic growth and technical change. They must draw these values from a limited historical experience containing several sharp shifts in trends for price, economic growth and oil quantities.

Chart 1
Oil Demand in Market Economies
1989 International Energy Outlook Price Path

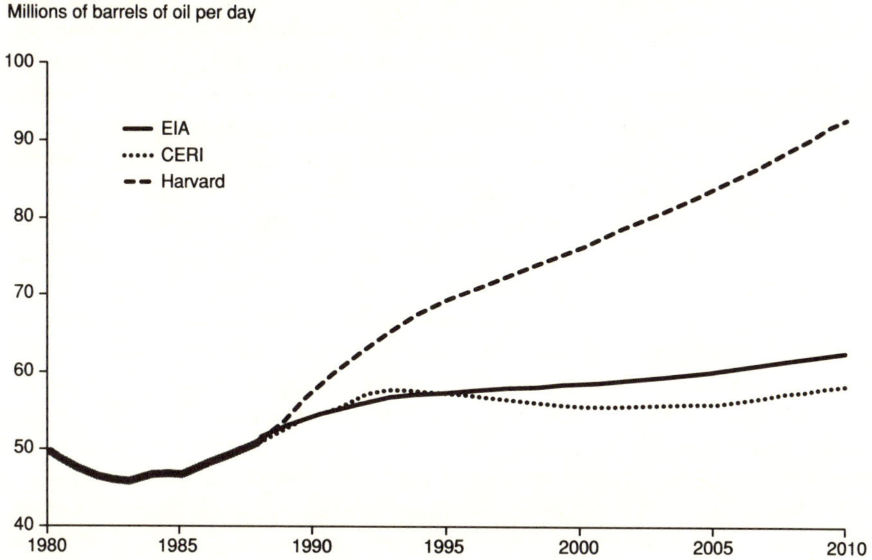

The higher oil consumption levels for the Harvard model reflect several conditions: (1) a stronger link between oil use and gross domestic product (GDP) that holds that a 1-percent increase in GDP results in a 1-percent increase in oil use, if oil prices remain unchanged; (2) the absence of autonomous efficiency improvements in oil use, unrelated to price, as new equipment replaces old equipment; and (3) adjustments in oil demand to previous price changes. Long-run oil intensities are dependent on only prices in this model. In the absence of higher prices, a long-run trend toward more efficient energy use does not exist. While some new technologies save energy, other technologies and lifestyle changes may actually use more energy. Moreover, because oil demand adjusts only gradually to price changes, the price declines during the late 1980s will continue to stimulate oil-demand growth during the 1990s, particularly if oil prices remain flat through the new decade.

The latter conclusion is evidenced clearly in the oil–GDP ratios for a scenario in which oil prices are assumed to remain flat at $19 per barrel through 2010. Chart 2 plots the results from all models without identifying each one (for ease of readability), with the 1988 value indexed to one. Most demand projections show that gains in oil intensity continue even without increased incentives for conserving oil. The oil-demand trends at the upper end of this group (indicating falling oil intensities) are consistent with the experiences of the late 1980s; those at the lower end of this range are consistent with the late-1970 trends.

Three models indicate that oil-demand intensities increase with flat oil prices. The Harvard model is joined by another model (the estimates by Steve Brown from the Federal Reserve Bank of Dallas) in showing rising oil intensity through 1995 before stabilizing through 2010. This spurt in oil demand, growing more rapidly than economic growth, reflects the adjustment in oil demand to post-1985 price changes, which were downward relative to prices in the 1970s and early 1980s. (The rising oil intensity in the third model occurs because flat prices in the future strongly stimulate demand.)

At the moment, it does not appear that the rise in oil intensities has happened to the degree indicated by the estimates at the higher end of this chart. However, it is important to know why. It could be that new technologies really are more energy efficient, regardless of price, even though such a trend has not yet been clearly detected in many of the statistical analyses of the historical experience. Alternatively, consumers may have viewed the price declines in the late 1980s as transitory rather than permanent and that investment in energy conservation still pays in the long run. If so, however, this possibility raises the intriguing prospect that world oil demands may grow briskly once consumers convince themselves that oil prices will remain flat over a number of years, as some observers of this market have projected.

Chart 2
Organization for Economic Cooperation and Development Oil–GDP Ratio, Flat Price Path

Alternative Perspectives on Oil Production

Estimates of oil production outside OPEC (excluding the Soviet Union) under these same oil-price assumptions also varied across models (*Chart 3*), although these differences are less pronounced than those for the market economies' demand. The vertical axis spans 60 million barrels per day in all charts showing oil quantities. In part, this smaller variation reflects that, while projected oil demands grow over the period, projected non-OPEC supplies fall or remain stable for the most part. Production grows in the Harvard estimates; it falls gradually in the EIA and CERI estimates.

Analysts agree that U.S. supplies will fall regardless of price assumptions because new reserves become increasingly expensive. Outside the United States, resource costs appear to be less important than institutional constraints on developing supplies; supplies in these regions either grow or remain stable.

Net U.S.S.R. exports could become an important new supply source and represent a significant uncertainty in any oil market outlook. In the current

Chart 3
Oil Supply Outside OPEC
1989 International Energy Outlook Price Path

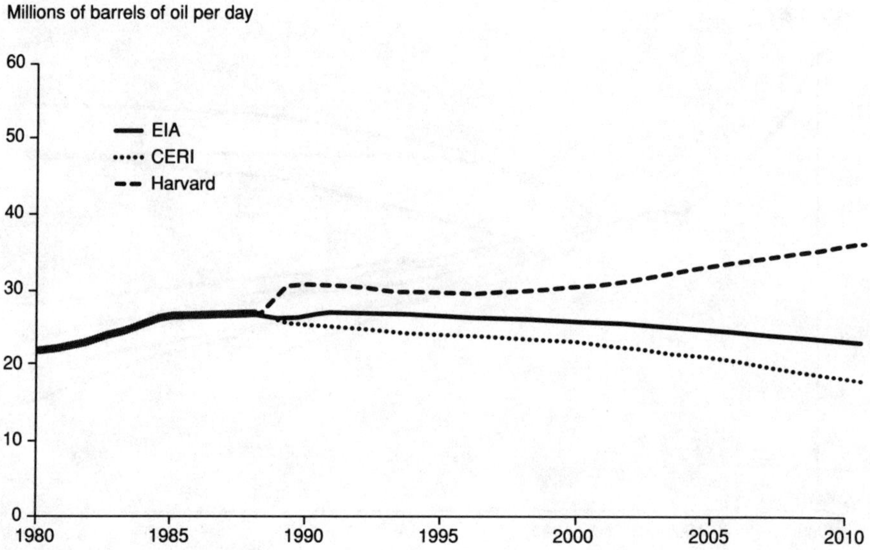

study, however, these exports do not vary much across models and, therefore, are not shown separately in this comparison.

Implications for the Call on OPEC

The call on OPEC under these same oil-price assumptions will equal the difference between total market demand minus production outside OPEC. Because market demands vary more across models than do non-OPEC supplies, differences in the call on OPEC will reflect differences in demand more than in non-OPEC supply. Thus, the net call on OPEC in Chart 4 is some 50 percent higher for Harvard, even though it indicated the highest non-OPEC production in the previous figure.

Market-Clearing Prices

In the previous charts, we compared total demand, non-OPEC production and the call on OPEC for a predetermined price path used by all modelers. In these estimates, OPEC was simply a passive producer, supplying any and all output to keep prices along the assumed long-run, sustained price path. We now ask a different question: Would OPEC be willing to produce this amount, and how would this output decision influence the market-clearing price in each model? Instead of fixing the price path and asking for the net demand for OPEC oil, we now ask for both price and OPEC's production.

Harvard's significantly higher net demand for OPEC oil in the previous 1989 IEO price case (*Chart 4*) should contribute to higher prices, as long as other factors do not offset this effect. But will the other two models, with lower net demands, indicate substantially lower prices? In Chart 4, CERI and EIA report very similar net demands for OPEC oil. But in Chart 5, with the market-clearing price, OPEC is willing to increase output much more readily in the CERI results than in EIA's. Output climbs steadily to 45 million barrels per day by 2010 in the CERI model but remains in the low 30-million-barrel-per-day level for the EIA and Harvard models.

Output decisions in the EIA and Harvard models are constrained by limits on OPEC capacity (about 37 million barrels per day) that reflect either economic or political objectives, including declining total net profits (appropriately

Chart 4
Call on OPEC
1989 International Energy Outlook Price Path

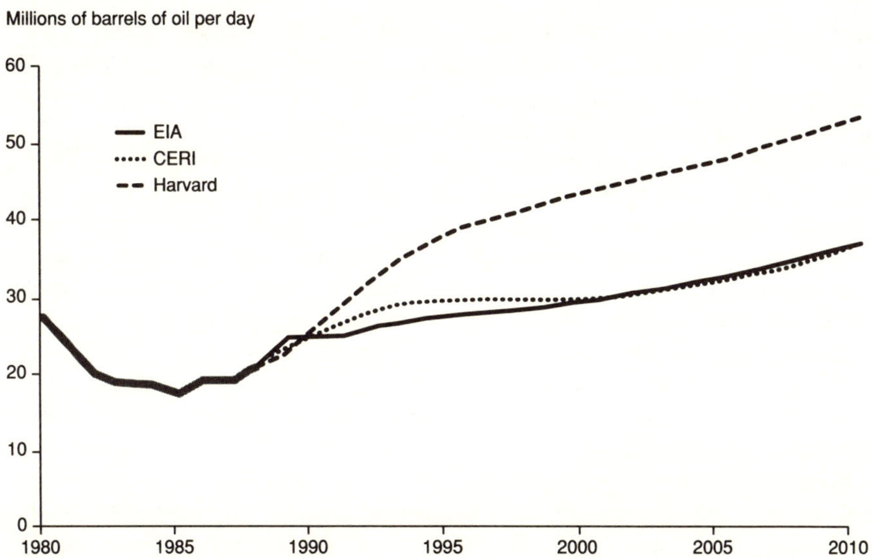

Chart 5
OPEC Production
Market-Clearing Price Case

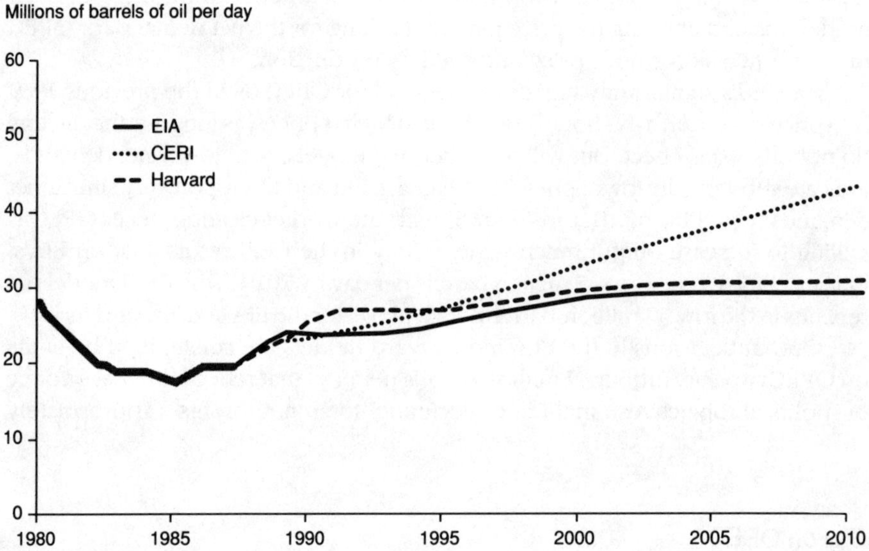

discounted) when sales exceed this limit, the ability to absorb additional oil revenues or a reluctance to sell more of a "patrimonial resource." The CERI results show either political constraints that are less binding or the opportunity to earn more net income, resulting in increased output.

Before discussing price, let us quickly review our progression. Initially, we showed that with a fixed price path the call on OPEC was much larger in the Harvard results than in the others because of the Harvard model's substantially higher total oil demand in the market economies; non-OPEC production did not vary as much across models. Next, we showed that with market-clearing prices, OPEC output was constrained to the low 30-million-barrel-per-day range in the EIA and Harvard results, while it rose to 45 million barrels per day in the CERI results.

Chart 6 plots the separate market-clearing price paths determined in each of the three models. It should be emphasized that these price paths resulted from standardized assumptions used by the modelers; their actual price projections based on their own assumptions may well be different. All prices rise through the decade but at considerably different rates. Low demand growth and expanding OPEC output keep CERI's prices along a low-growth track, increasing to the low $20s by 2000 and to about $30 by 2010. This path is representative of the median response in the July 1990 International Energy Workshop poll reported by Manne and Schrattenholzer (1990). Harvard's rapid demand growth coupled with constrained OPEC output translates into sharply higher prices. Although demand grows much more slowly in the EIA projections, constrained OPEC production eventually forces prices to track Harvard's. Across all models, when OPEC output is below the mid-35-million-barrel-per-day level, prices are always considerably higher than $30 in this scenario.

Thus, low prices are associated with both low demand growth and expanded OPEC production. If either or both of these conditions do not hold, substantially higher prices result. These benchmarks should be useful for evaluating other price projections. If one expects constant prices through the next two decades, what are the demand trends that accompany that projection? Given reasonable bounds on production outside the cartel, what are the implications for OPEC's need to expand capacity at these prices?

Collectively, the modelers participating in our study were suspicious of the flat oil-price world (at $19 per barrel through 2010). Chart 7 shows the mean

Chart 6
World Oil Price
Market-Clearing Price Case

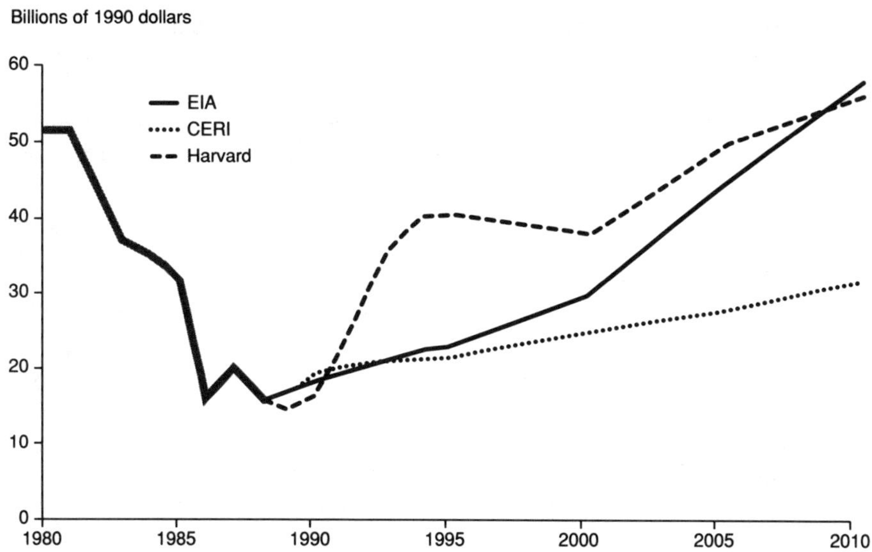

Chart 7
Source of Oil Supplies
Flat Price Path

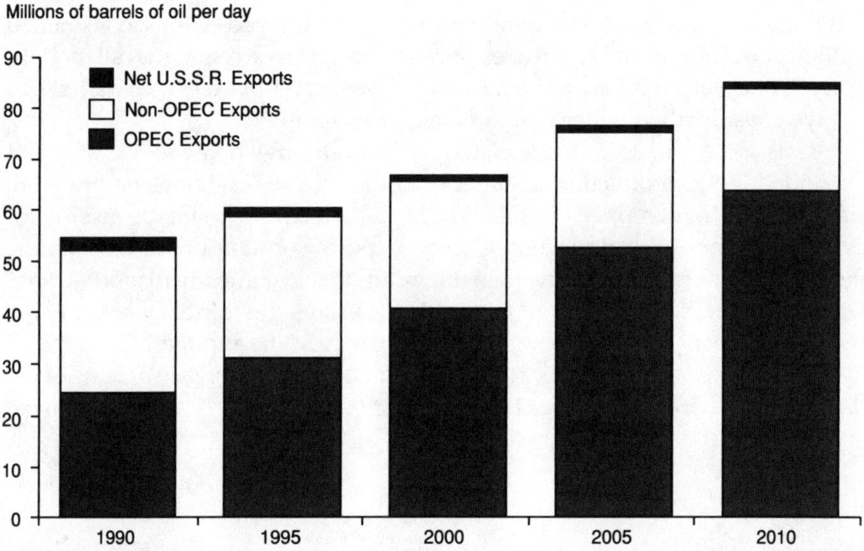

results from all models based on such a price path. Total market economy demand is shown as the sum of three supply sources: OPEC, non-OPEC and net U.S.S.R. exports. Total demand grows from about 50 million barrels per day to 65 million barrels per day over the next decade. Because of modestly declining non-OPEC production, OPEC production would need to expand to 40 million barrels per day, or increase by 6 percent per year. A decrease in market economies' economic growth of 1 percentage point per year reduces the call on OPEC to 34 million barrels per day; an increase in economic growth of that magnitude raises the call on OPEC to 46 million barrels per day.

I do not interpret Chart 7 as necessarily ruling out flat prices through the decade, but only as showing the necessary conditions for such a price path. OPEC could physically expand output to meet such demands if it desired. Perhaps current assessments of non-OPEC production (reflected in the mean results) are too pessimistic by 1 million to 2 million barrels per day. Alternatively, aggressive demand management programs also could chip away at this call on OPEC. It becomes much more difficult, however, to extend this price path through the next two decades without an explicit assumption that new

Chart 8
U.S. Supply and Demand
Flat and Rising Price Paths

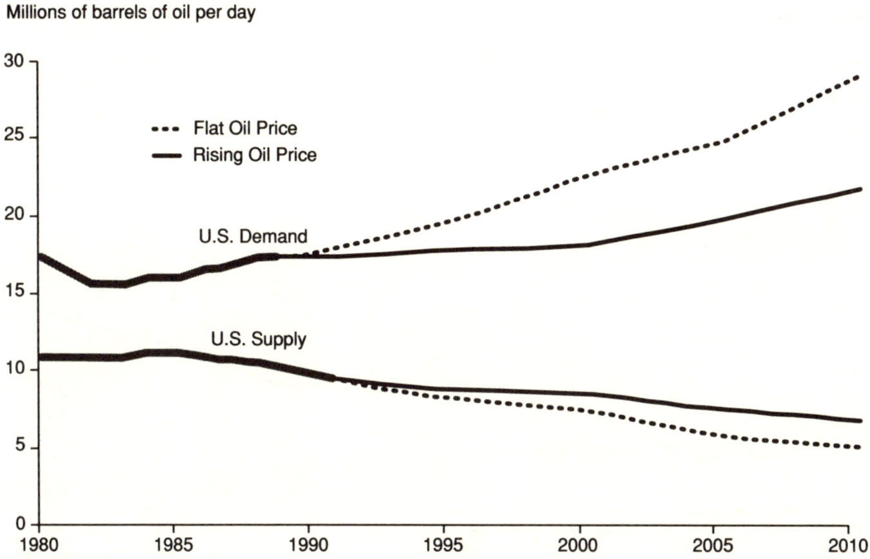

technologies will introduce alternative fuels at low prices and in great abundance.

Growing Dependence on Persian Gulf Oil

Despite substantial differences in supplies, demands and prices, there is an agreement across models and scenarios that the world economy will become increasingly more dependent on Persian Gulf oil over the next decade. Currently, more than 40 percent of the market economies' oil demand originates in OPEC countries. The average share projected in the study rises to 55 percent in 2000 and 60 percent in 2010 in the 1989 IEO price case. Symptomatic of this development, U.S. oil imports grow in all scenarios and models. And the oil-import bill more than doubles in many instances.

Rising U.S. oil imports will not be altered easily. Chart 8 compares the average U.S. oil consumption and production in the flat $19-per-barrel case and in the rising price case (to $39 per barrel by 2000 and flat thereafter). Higher prices clearly reduce oil consumption growth and slow the decline in oil production, but the

Chart 9
U.S. Imports
Flat and Rising Price Paths

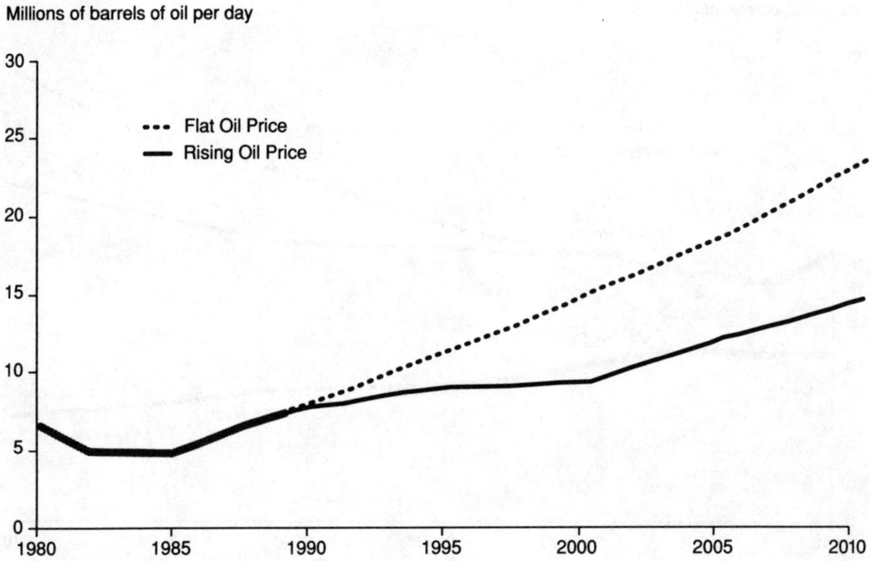

need for imports grows, as witnessed in Chart 9. This growing need occurs despite a doubling in the U.S. price, which could increase because of a higher world oil price or domestic U.S. policies that raise the price above world levels. Thus, Chart 9 indicates the difficulty and costliness of reducing imports enough to significantly alter the nation's exposure to oil imports or the insecurity of the world's oil supply. Because of this high cost and great difficulty, appropriate policy responses should include efforts to help the economy adapt to future price shocks. Such strategies might include oil stockpiles and macroeconomic stabilization policies.

References

Energy Modeling Forum (1991), "International Oil Supplies and Demands," *EMF Report 11* (Stanford, Calif.: Stanford University, September) forthcoming.

Manne, Alan S., and Leo Schrattenholzer (1990), "International Energy Workshop: Overview of Poll Responses," International Energy Project (Stanford, Calif.: Stanford University, Department of Operations Research, July).

Exploration and Development in the 1990s: Impact on the Southwest

Isaac C. Kerridge, Jr.

I would like to talk a little about some aspects of the energy industry that have an impact directly on the economy of the Southwest. Exploration for and development of oil and gas have a significant impact on the Southwest economy. The area that comprises the Eleventh Federal Reserve District, plus Oklahoma, is an important consumer of oil-field equipment and services. In 1988, drilling expenditures in this area amounted to more than $4.6 billion, or 43.8 percent of the total U.S. expenditure for drilling. At the end of October, this same area had 580 rotary rigs drilling, or 52 percent of the U.S. total of 1,107 rigs.

The same area is very important as a producer of oil-field machinery. According to the 1987 *Census of Manufactures*, which is the most current numbers we have, 69 percent (by value) of U.S. shipments of oil and gas drilling equipment emanated from plants located in this same area of the Eleventh District, and the number exceeds 75 percent if you include Oklahoma.

I wish to briefly cover two topics. First, what are the major determinants for drilling and the outlook for each of those? Second, how does the outlook for oil drilling differ from that of natural gas drilling?

Five Major Determinants for Drilling Activity

Probably the most important determinant of drilling is the difference between price and finding costs. Two panelists have already illustrated some of the difficulties in trying to predict oil and gas prices. In our company, we expect volatility around a rising price trend. But I will point out that it is a rising trend from pre-August price levels, not from current levels. It is also likely that the discount from oil at which natural gas currently sells will be reduced over the coming decade.

According to Arthur Andersen's *Eleventh Survey of Oil and Gas Reserve Disclosures*, U.S. finding costs have declined in four of the past five years and in 1989 were 3 percent below foreign finding costs. Why, then, do major companies seem to be shifting their exploration activities abroad? I think the answer lies in where large reserves remain to be discovered. Now if this trend of lower finding costs continues and if we are correct about the direction of prices, then this first determinant of drilling is clearly a positive.

The second factor or determinant in drilling is the need to replace production with new reserve additions. This need is clearly a stimulus to exploration and the acquisition of reserves. For an oil company to allow reserves to decline for any extended period signals to the financial community essentially a decision to leave the business. So, management is concerned with reserve levels, and that tends to maintain or increase exploratory activity. (Almost without exception, the owners of the world's large reserves are national oil companies. The largest reserves, of course, are held by Aramco.)

A third determinant of drilling is new technology. New technology can trigger increased drilling. Two recent, significant developments in this area are 3-D seismic with improved interpretation and recent innovations to allow completion of horizontally drilled wells.

In January 1989, Texas Railroad Commission District 1, which is the area around San Antonio and to the south, had an average of one rotary rig running. In October 1990, District 1 had an average of 74 rotary rigs drilling largely horizontal holes.

We estimate that by the year 2000 at least 5,000 horizontal wells will be drilled, representing an annual growth rate of almost 20 percent. We are convinced that this will be the fastest-growing segment of domestic drilling.

Another determinant of drilling is tax policy. Back in the 1920s, Congress provided tax incentives that recognized the risk and the unique aspects of petroleum exploration. Subsequently, the larger companies lost the depletion allowance. Then the Tax Reform Act of 1986 effectively canceled the remaining incentives for most independents. Whether Congress realized what they were doing is hard to say, but that was the net effect of the alternative minimum tax. Recent events in the Persian Gulf and the monumental costs of protecting oil sources in that region cast doubt on the wisdom of this 1986 act. Unless Congress can be convinced that domestic drilling benefits all consumers in the entire nation, this determinant is not likely to become positive. The recent budget agreement changes the alternative minimum tax treatment of intangible drilling costs and percentage depletion allowance for some marginally producing properties. It also made a few other minor changes that will tend to increase the incentive for domestic drilling. These changes, included in the recent budget legislation, are likely to result in about a 5-percent increase in U.S. drilling over the next several years.

The final significant determinant of drilling involves access to productive areas. The United States is a rather mature petroleum province. We have been exploring for more than 100 years. Most of the giant oil fields under accessible land have already been found. Most sizable remaining reserves lie offshore in Alaska and under federal lands in the West.

While one would not argue with protecting environmentally sensitive areas, the oil companies have shown that they can offer that protection. Most ludicrous are prohibitions on offshore drilling under the banner of protecting the environment. Consider these facts: 1.5 percent of ocean pollution around the United States over an extended period of time has come from offshore drilling; 45 percent of ocean pollution in the same period can be traced to oil tankers. Our prohibition of offshore drilling greatly increases the risk of pollution as more tankers bring in more oil, unless, of course, everyone is willing to revert to bicycles and wooden stoves—and even the wooden stoves would not do great things for the environment.

The largest natural gas field east of the Mississippi River is believed to lie off the coast of North Carolina, but it cannot be developed even though it is rather difficult to imagine having an oil spill from a gas pipeline.

Will logic prevail? I do not know, but this factor is likely to remain a negative.

U.S. Drilling Prospects Favor Natural Gas

The second topic involves the differing outlook for oil and natural gas. A high percentage of perspective lands onshore in the United States have already been drilled in varying depths in search of oil and gas. In many areas, however, not many deep wells—wells drilled to depths of 15,000 feet or more—have been drilled. Because hydrocarbons deeper than 15,000 feet are more likely to be in the gaseous form, remaining U.S. exploration at deeper levels will favor natural gas.

The determination of ultimately recoverable oil and gas reserves is still an inexact science. The magnitude of reserves in place is an estimate, and recoverability is influenced by both economics and technology. Within technical limits, the percentage of oil and gas that can be recovered is positively correlated with price. Now with this disclaimer, most experts believe that the resource base for natural gas in the United States is greater than that for oil.

Proved recoverable crude-oil reserves in the United States are approximately 27 billion barrels, or about a nine-year supply at current production rates. New technologies, such as horizontal drilling, may increase the percentage of oil reserves that are recoverable.

Current proved recoverable natural gas reserves at current prices are estimated at 161 trillion cubic feet, or just less than a nine-year supply at current production rates. So, our reserve-production ratio for oil and natural gas is currently about the same. But at prices ranging from $3 to $5 per million cubic feet, reserves of natural gas increase to about 277 trillion cubic feet, or a 15-year supply. Estimates of ultimately recoverable reserves of natural gas range as high as 800 trillion cubic feet, or 40 times current annual production. Some of that may not be economical, though, at foreseeable prices.

Another reason that natural gas is expected to be the fuel of the future is the heightened concern for the environment. The Clean Air Act recently passed by Congress will result in some substitution of natural gas for coal. And with nuclear power on hold, most of the nation's incremental electric power generating capacity is coming from gas-fired cogeneration units.

The South Coast Air Quality Management District of California, with a growing population—they expect the population to grow about 40 percent in the next 20 years—and with an ambitious goal of air quality improvement, will almost certainly have to mandate widespread conversion of vehicles to compressed natural gas fuel if they have any hope of attaining their air pollution goals.

The move is already underway for mass transit and larger fleets, but the politicians have not been willing to tackle the individual driver. But for these and other reasons, we believe that in the 1990s the emphasis will be on discovering and developing additional natural gas reserves, including the recovery of methane gas from underground coal seams. This effort was fairly strong this past year in anticipation of the possible elimination of a government subsidy to coal seam gas at the end of 1990, but Congress extended the subsidy for two years. Actually, the measure may result in slightly fewer wells being drilled next year now that the pressure to complete wells in the calendar year 1990 is off.

Conclusion

In summary, recent events in the Persian Gulf have given us a second lesson in the importance of secure domestic energy sources. Our best chance of enhancing our domestic energy position lies in developing natural gas resources. Because of the concentration of oil-field equipment and service industry and of natural gas pipelines in the Southwest, and because of the area's importance as a producer of oil and gas, this effort should contribute to the prosperity of the Southwestern economy.

I guess I cannot end without some sort of forecast, but I should explain that we really do not make long-range forecasts. We forecast a couple of years for business-planning purposes, but I guess we would agree with other speakers you have heard that the volatility of oil prices and the uncertainty surrounding those prices is so great that it really makes it difficult to forecast very far in the future.

Recognizing the tentative nature of any oil-price forecast until the course of events in the Persian Gulf region becomes known, we have based our 1991 drilling forecast on a rather conservative projection of $23 per barrel, average 1991 price for West Texas Intermediate crude. Natural gas at the wellhead is forecast at an average of $1.85 per million cubic feet in 1991, up about 12 percent from the expected average price this year but down from the current price, which is in anticipation of the heating season. With these price assumptions, our growing model forecasts an average U.S. rig count in 1991 of 1,160, up 14.7 percent from the 1990 average or estimate of 1,011. In 1992, we anticipate about an additional 12-percent increase in domestic drilling. Our forecast for foreign activity is for smaller increases this year but an overall increase in worldwide drilling activity, as measured by the rig count, of about 12 percent next year. This forecast, while less than half of the 2,500 rigs that this country needs to employ to actually arrest the decline in U.S. crude production, does indicate continued improvement for this sector of the Southwest economy.

Oil in the 1990s: Boom or Bust?

Edward N. Krapels

Any long-term view of the oil market must be through the keyhole of current events. A long, extensive war in the Persian Gulf in 1990 and 1991 will lead to a different world than a negotiated settlement with Iraq will. In these circumstances, for the purpose of long-term analysis, it is most useful to identify the deepest underlying trends influencing oil, analyze these trends and make judgments about their course in the 1990s.

In this process, Energy Security Analysis Inc. (ESAI) has developed a view of the future that we can best sum up as follows:

- **The politics of oil supply.** The Middle East will be even more chronically unstable in the 1990s than in the 1980s. Early in the 1990s, there will be little spare production capacity (we assume Kuwait will be severely damaged during the war), and prices will periodically exceed $30 per barrel as new turmoil roils the Middle Eastern regimes.
- **The politics of oil demand.** This instability will cause governments to reinvigorate anti-oil demand policies that will put world oil demand—and the call on the Organization of Petroleum Exporting Countries (OPEC)—on a substantially lower growth path.
- **The timing of price pressures.** This return to very low oil-demand growth will not happen immediately. Even though the recession will make oil demand lower in 1991 than in 1990, oil demand is likely to pick up in 1992 because there is still such a strong growth bias for oil in the world economy (especially in developing countries, including Eastern Europe). The anti-oil-demand policies implemented in 1991 only gradually will have a strong effect on demand.
- **On-the-swing producer.** It is still OPEC. We see non-OPEC supply remaining flat in the 1992–95 period. Thus, any growth in oil demand in 1992–95 must be supplied by OPEC. OPEC meetings will continue to be the only mechanism that attempts to balance supply and demand.

Sometimes it will work; sometimes it will not.

- **The change in industry structure.** Partial and haphazard vertical integration by OPEC members will only promote additional competition.
- **The financial balance of power.** The Iraq crisis of 1990–91 restored OPEC financial flows to levels reminiscent of the good old days of 1979–80. Under normal circumstances, such a windfall could substantially change the balance of the oil industry's financial power. The need to re-arm and rebuild, however, will prevent the Middle Eastern countries from using the oil wealth within the oil market and the oil industry. Put another way, the wealth will *not* be used to consolidate the Middle East's oil-supply dominance. Put yet another way, Saudi Arabia will never produce much more than 10 million barrels of oil per day.

In developing a reasonable view of the long term, it is impossible to overemphasize the importance of the politics of oil. Without politics, the Middle East today would be producing 30 million barrels of oil; it is their comparative advantage, and only the chronic intrusion of political events keeps a lid on the world's appetite for the region's oil. Thus, any long-term analysis of the oil market must be rooted, first and foremost, in a political framework. How will international politics work out the Middle East conflicts?

The Political Outlook

Oil affairs have always had heavy political undertones, essentially because governments have viewed disruptions in oil supply and prices as sufficiently important to constitute a national interest. This has always been true of countries—such as OPEC members—who earn the bulk of their foreign exchange and national incomes from oil. OPEC's very existence is the result. It is also true of countries that import oil. Even though there was widespread deregulation of oil markets in the 1980s, it remains true that when oil supplies are seriously threatened, governments intervene. Paul Frankel's reconstruction of a famous phrase—that oil is too important to be left to oilmen—remains sporadically valid. The defense of Kuwait and Saudi Arabia is telling evidence; were they not the repositories of a good fraction of the world's oil reserves, the United States and its allies would not have confronted Saddam Hussein.

The central fact remains that the bulk of the world's petroleum reserves are in the Middle East, one of the most inherently unstable political regions in the world. The situation boils down to this: *as we live through the agonies of one political crisis, however it ends, we can be virtually certain that another crisis will arise in the 1990s.*

This prospect *should* cause governments of oil-importing countries to the future. Before Iraq invaded Kuwait, a growing consensus maintained that crude oil prices would strengthen and, because of constraints on refinery construction in most parts of the developed world, that finished product prices would rise even more. ESAI's analysis casts doubts on both these perceptions.

Investment in crude-oil production capacity must be seen in the context of two different sets of economics: those faced by the management of oil companies and those faced by the leadership of oil-exporting countries. We have no doubt that oil companies will continue to invest in exploration and production, but we believe the price at which projects will have to be profitable will remain well below the $30-per-barrel level seen after the Iraqi invasion. We believe most companies still will require oil development projects to come in at less than $20 per barrel.

Even more important is the investment attitudes of the governments of oil-exporting countries. Before the invasion of Kuwait, we expected substantial expansion of capacity in the Persian Gulf countries. Vast sums now must be spent to return Kuwait to its precrisis capacity. Iraq will be anathema to foreign investors and bank lending for years to come. One of the deepest consequences of the crisis is that the vast oil potential of Iraq may never be realized.

That brings us to Saudi Arabia. The long-term future of oil may well rest on the Saudis' willingness to develop a productive capacity to match their awesome reserve size of, say, 15 million barrels per day. If they do, they can obtain a decisive leadership role in oil affairs, a role they abandoned in 1985. One has to question, however, the willingness and the ability of the Saudi regime to make such an investment. However the conflict with Iraq is resolved, growing claims on Saudi revenues will come from several sources:

- Defense expenditures will rise as the Saudis beef up against further conflict with Iraq or other adversaries.
- Gifts and loans to other Arab countries and causes must rise to purchase, or perhaps *lease* is a better word, acceptance of the tremendous income and wealth disparities between Saudis and other Arabs.
- Some segments of Saudi leadership may want to lay claim to part of the revenue stream for external investments to enable the Saudis to have a wealthy government in exile, as the Kuwaitis have been able to maintain.

These competing claims for money are likely to make the head of state and his closest advisors feel cash-poor. This is hardly conducive to making very large investments in a substantial expansion of oil production capacity whose very existence would result in lower prices.

The primary mechanisms for what might be called strategic or long-term risk management are

- vertical integration among companies that produce and refine oil,

prepare for another crisis. To the extent they do prepare, oil prices in the 19 will be lower, and the economic consequences of the next crisis will be le severe. To the extent they do not prepare for the next crisis, oil prices will b higher and the consequences will be more severe.

There are, then, two sets of political forces we must observe: the forces acting to destabilize the Middle East, and hence the supply of oil, and the corresponding reactive forces influencing governments of oil-importing countries to lower their demand for oil.

ESAI's assumptions about these two forces, and thus the basis of its long-term market view, are as follows:

- The Middle East will experience additional and repeated political upheavals, some involving revolutions within nations and others involving conflict between nations.
- Oil-importing countries will initially be reluctant to implement strong additional anti-oil-demand policies. Importing countries may try new security frameworks. But as the instability persists, oil importers' willingness to strengthen oil conservation and substitution programs will grow.

In this fashion, the developed countries will gradually recreate an anti-growth bias in their oil economies, which will be visible via decoupling of oil-demand growth from economic growth. (Put another way, the oil use per dollar of gross national product (GNP) will fall.)

Developing countries will therefore constitute the incremental demand market. When oil was cheap (1986–90), their demand grew very rapidly. The high prices during the Iraq crisis will force developing countries to curtail demand. Ironically, however, the financial hardships caused by the oil-price rise also will prevent these countries from investing in alternative fuel sources. Thus, when oil prices come down again, less-developed countries will increase oil demand.

With these assumptions, we believe the politics of the oil market of the 1990s will initially produce tight supply and fairly high prices, with high probability of another supply disruption. Then, in the mid-1990s, anti-oil-demand policies and development of alternative supplies will re-create substantial spare capacity and, consequently, strong downward pressure on prices. Demand for oil will pick up again in developing countries, but anti-oil bias will keep its demand growth low in the industrial world.

The Financial Aspects

Another important but often neglected part of a long-term oil market outlook is the investment climate created by bullish or bearish perceptions of

- financialization of aspects of the business through swaps, royalty trusts and other mechanisms,
- vertical disintegration to subject each facet of the business to the discipline of the capital markets and
- reregulation or other forms of intervention, such as large subsidies or alternatives to importing oil, by governments for whom the risk has become too big to handle.

All these mechanisms affect the structure, operations and degree of competition within the oil industry. The most fundamentally important mechanism is the degree and pace of vertical integration by oil-exporting countries. In recent years, we have seen several major oil-exporting nations (including besieged Kuwait) make major moves downstream. Some analysts have suggested that this could create a new era for the oil market and industry. Will it?

Unique or the New Norm?

We tend to think of the future in terms of the past. Long-term forecasts often, indeed usually, simply project into the future the present industry structure, the present political framework and the present set of financial relationships and then impose into that projection of the present a set of supply and demand analyses that are sure to be wrong.

In so doing, we turn what is sure to be a unique new situation into generally acceptable scenarios of supply, demand and price. Before we present our supply-demand scenarios, which suffer from the same generality, we want to emphasize that we believe that oil in the 1990s has unique qualities. There may be no growth in demand despite low prices, there may be widespread integration between producers and consumers with more, not less, intense competition, and there may be changes in long-established governments. These events will provide the framework in which oil supply, demand and price will sort themselves. And oil supply, demand and price will, in turn, affect the broader framework of world events. That is the complex reality.

PART FIVE

The Future of the Southwest Economy

"Over the longer term, I see several factors that have the potential to boost economic growth in this region relative to the rest of the country."

—Harvey Rosenblum

"Education really is the answer to what we are facing in the future.... We must begin to think now, immediately, about investing in the young people who are in our schools today."

—Kathryn Whitmire

"[T]he most growth-enhancing types of expenditures are the ones that should be focused on."

—William Gruben

"We have got to improve the environmental situation in the state."

—Tom Luce

"In three of the four major areas of state obligation and responsibility, we are operating in this state more or less in a crisis fashion."

—Dan Morales

"As fatiguing as it would be to have the Legislature in session on a regular basis every year, I think there is a need for a move in that direction."

— Diana Natalicio

The Southwest Economy: A Prologue for the Future

Harvey Rosenblum

"Life must be lived forwards but can only be understood backwards."
—Kierkegaard

To understand what is happening in the Southwest economy today and what will happen in the future, it is imperative that we understand what happened here in the past. A good place to begin is to examine the past decade and the events that shaped economic developments in the Southwest. If we considered the 10 most important economic events of the 1980s in the United States, we would find that about seven of them were also of major importance for the Southwest and, in fact, continue to play an important role in shaping the 1990s.

In my discussion this morning, I am going to cover many topics, but before I do, let me state my conclusion at the outset: the economy of this region is finally headed in the right direction. Two years ago at this conference I presented a similar long-term economic outlook, and I could not say with confidence that we were headed in the right direction. Now I can say so with confidence.

I will first examine the region's near-term outlook based on what is happening nationally and its effects on the Southwest. Then I will turn to the long-term influences shaping the region's economy. I will explain several reasons to be optimistic about the future but will note several critical public-policy decisions that lie ahead and could have a great bearing on the Southwest's future.

Based on current economic indicators, the Southwest economy will outperform the United States' economy over the next few years. Yet, the decisions we make today could mean that, instead of outperforming the nation, the region will backtrack and underperform the nation. To understand the choices we confront now, let's look back to the 1980s and the factors that shaped that decade.

Top Economic Events of the 1980s

Since about 1989, I have been describing the Southwest's experience during the 1980s as the Great Recession. It was not a depression, at least not on the scale of the 1930s. I use the term *Great Recession* because the Southwest's experience in the 1980s was by no means an ordinary recession. What the region experienced was somewhere between a recession and a depression. If I had to pick which end of the spectrum it was closer to, the history of the 1980s for this region was closer to depression than to recession. Had it not been for people like Bob Boykin [former Dallas Fed president], the economy might have slipped further toward depression than it did.

In looking at the 1980s, it is helpful to remember a concept from business-cycle theory: every boom, every great expansion in the economy also carries with it the seeds of the next recession. Booms—and the 1970s for this region of the country were a boom—usually contain the seeds of a big bust. Economist Joseph Schumpeter many years ago said that one aspect of capitalism is that it carries with it the seeds of creative destruction. What he meant, I think, was that recessions renew things. In the Southwest, we are beginning to see the seeds of the next expansion take root; we are beginning to see the flowers come up above the ground. Nowhere is this more true than in the energy industry.

Oil prices. With the gyration of oil prices, this region experienced a boom-and-bust cycle in the energy business over the past decade. As a proportion of the District's economic output, energy went from about 21 percent of the value of output—a little bit more than one-fifth—to a little bit less than one-tenth of the region's economic output. In short, energy became half as important to this area of the country as it once was. The decline, of course, had spillover effects. The lower prices boosted petrochemicals and provided a premium to the high-tech and human-capital-intensive part of the oil business—the seeds of expansion, the use of brain power.

Regional deflation. The nation went from a period of inflation in the 1970s to a period of disinflation in the 1980s. Nationally, the consumer price index went from 13 percent at the start of the 1980s to 4 percent to 5 percent in the period from 1984 to 1989. But trends in the Southwest were not that way at all. We went through regional and sectoral deflation—not disinflation, but deflation.

As a result of the region's deflation, a lot of goods and services here are cheap relative to other parts of the country, which makes us a relatively attractive place to do business—another example of the seeds of expansion.

Tax reform. The Economic Recovery Tax Act of 1981 provided all kinds of special incentives to real estate investment, encouraging diversification out of energy lending and into real estate lending by our banking industry. Then the Tax Reform

Act of 1986 unwound all the prior incentives and reinforced the regional downward spiral that accompanied the plummeting oil prices that year. The net impact was that these changes in tax laws created unnecessary instability. I do not want to say that there are any seeds for recovery in all the tax reform we have been through. I view those reforms as just policy direction going one way and then the other way and just creating unnecessary instability. Nonetheless, tax reform was an important set of events because it affected the timing of our regional downturn and reinforced the way our economy was out of phase with that of the nation.

Federal budget deficit. The federal budget deficit was accompanied by an increase in the relative importance of defense spending. Actually, that increased spending helped stabilize the economy here in the District over the past several years. But going into the 1990s, we are a bit weaker than other parts of the country because that buildup in defense spending left less money available from the federal government for infrastructure at a time when our state and local governments, unlike those in many other regions, were cramped for funds. So, our infrastructure is a weakness.

Financial deregulation. Throughout the United States, financial deregulation provided our financial institutions with new funding abilities in the 1980s. We gave them access to national markets for insured deposits. That changed the whole structure of the industry for both banks and thrifts. We gave thrifts new investment powers for real estate and for corporate junk bonds. We gave financial institutions, particularly thrifts, deregulation accompanied by de-supervision. *De-supervision* is probably not a word you have heard of, but it basically is a lot less supervision than they should have had. The result of all this became another big event of the 1980s: bank and thrift failures.

Bank and thrift failures. Without going through a lot of historical details, let me just say that, according to Dallas Fed statistics, the bank failure rate in Texas in the 1980s was worse than what was experienced in the 1930s. For banking, real estate and a few related industries, there is no question that the decade of the 1980s was a depression.

For a couple of years now, I have been saying that the only thing unique about the banking and thrift collapse in Texas and the Southwest was that it happened here first. Accompanying that collapse was a credit crunch of unforeseen proportions. Basically what the credit crunch did was to serve as a major impediment to growth, even if it was not of sufficient strength to, by itself, put the Southwest economy in reverse. At this time [November 1990], the banking industry, in terms of the credit it is providing to the economy, is about in neutral. And I think it is about to head into first gear. I am reasonably confident that the banking industry in the Eleventh District, instead of being an impediment to growth, soon will become a major support force for economic growth—again, the seeds of expansion.

The value of the dollar. Another economic event that had an impact on this region was the value of the dollar. It reinforced other sources of economic instability. The dollar weakened our manufacturing in the early 1980s, and it boosted our manufacturing, agriculture and other exporting industries around 1987 and thereafter.

Additional factors. Three other economic events of the 1980s that were significant nationally were of less importance in explaining the Southwest's Great Recession. These are the Dow Jones Average stock market index, the very sharp demographic changes during the decade, especially in the labor force, and the destruction of the Berlin Wall, which, as Chairman Greenspan indicated yesterday, will have a major impact in the 1990s.

The Near-Term Economic Outlook for the Southwest

Having covered the past, let's turn to the outlook for the Southwest economy for the next few years. To do that, we must look at the national economy, which is experiencing a confluence of at least three interrelated economic shocks. One shock came in oil prices; one came in credit availability, and the third—the result of the first two shocks—will probably be a national recession. These three forces, I think, increase the usual degree of uncertainty that accompanies any economic forecast. As Admiral Bobby Inman said at the opening of the conference yesterday, "There's more uncertainty on the horizon as I look ahead than at any time in my adult life." Admiral Inman was referring to the national and international outlook in his statement.

However, in the Southwest region, the outlines of the future are more clearly evident. They may be hazy, but they certainly seem clearer now than when we held this conference in 1988. Four factors that are now influencing the national economy will also trickle down to affect the Southwest economy: oil prices, the credit crunch, tax reform and monetary policy.

Oil prices. The Dallas Fed's November 1990 issue of *Southwest Economy* summarized our assessment of the impact of higher oil prices. The long and short of our position is that oil prices above $30 per barrel are sufficient to produce a national recession, and given the nation's sluggish rate of growth in August 1990—before the invasion of Kuwait—this is probably enough to tip the economy over the edge toward recession. The higher oil prices rise and the longer they persist, the longer and deeper will be the recession.

The Persian Gulf crisis has resulted in the loss of Iraqi and Kuwaiti oil in world markets. Before the crisis, oil from the two countries represented about 8 percent of free-world consumption. Other countries, especially Saudi Arabia and Mexico, have increased production to offset the losses. Overall, we have lost about 2 percent to 3 percent of the free-world oil supply, which is a significant amount.

What impact will this have in the Southwest? We benefit from higher energy prices, but not initially. We probably will not see any real benefits until possibly June 1991, and *only then* if oil prices remain high. But in the meantime, we will be suffering the effects of the U.S. recession. Companies that export to national and international markets, such as our computer and telecommunications firms, will be hurt. They will get the bad news before they get the good news. The medium-term impact is that in the second half of 1991 we will probably start to generate some job growth if oil prices remain high. However, at yesterday afternoon's session you heard from four energy-industry experts who said that prices may not remain high; they will fluctuate and may actually go down. The long-run impact of high oil prices in Texas alone could mean the creation of more than 200,000 jobs over the next several years. But sustained high prices are not expected until the middle of the decade when OPEC basically starts to run out of capacity. So, I think the initial impact of higher oil prices is not necessarily good for the District.

Credit crunch. A national credit crunch is now making front-page headlines. The U.S. economy probably was headed toward recession, or was weak, before the Persian Gulf crisis. Higher oil prices may be enough to tip the economy into recession, but one of the factors contributing to that weakness is the spreading national credit crunch. The credit crunch and the weak economy will begin to reinforce one another, which will depress bank earnings.

When bank earnings get depressed, banks tend to lend less, so there will be some credit shrinkage. Texas bank loans went from a high of about $125 billion in 1985 to a low of about $78 billion in 1990. Basically, Texas sustained a 40 percent loss in its volume of credit. More recently, credit levels have begun to stabilize, but volume still seems to be shrinking a little bit.

If New England gets a credit shrinkage of only one-fourth or one-third that magnitude, the credit shrinkage will reinforce the downturn that the region is already experiencing. New England's strength, which came from sizeable credit expansion in the past few years, was sowing the seeds for the destruction that would follow later.

1990 tax reform. We have just been through the budget summit. It came at a bad time because people were already uncertain because of higher oil prices and the credit outlook. The budget summit added to the uncertainty and the depressed household and business confidence that was already extant in the economy because of energy and banking. In this case, tax reform contains virtually no spending impetus or income-creating incentives. Most of the impact simply will be higher taxes. One notable exception is the small tax-based initiative for energy exploration that the 1990 tax reform included.

Monetary policy. Monetary policy, by the Fed's own admission, for the past couple of years has been leaning against the wind, trying to fight upward inflationary pressures in what amounted to a fairly booming economic environment. The economic environment in the past couple of years, at least according to the employment statistics, was full-out full employment. Full employment tends to be a little more inflationary than less-than-full employment.

We had our rude awakening this summer when the gross national product statistics for the past couple of years were revised. Instead of seeing the economy growing at 3 percent to 4 percent as we had thought it had been growing, we learned that the economy had been growing at 1-percent to 2-percent annual rates for the past couple of years.

We have to rely on the statistics available at the time monetary-policy decisions are made. But in retrospect, I would conclude that had we had the right statistics at the time, we would have had a slightly different monetary policy. Monetary policy, inadvertently, was probably a little tighter than we intended, which created another slowing force in the economy. (I am referring only to the year or two prior to the GNP revisions released in July 1990; I am neither commenting about current monetary policy nor predicting what monetary will be in the future.)

Putting these four factors together—higher oil prices, a credit crunch, tax reform and monetary policy that was a little tighter than it probably should have been—the United States and the Southwest may be in for some rough sledding unless we find a peaceful solution in the Middle East, and unless it can be found very quickly. To use Admiral Inman's words, we are skating on the edge of a recession.

The economy probably will be a lot worse in the United States as a whole than in the Southwest. The Southwest will get some offsetting benefit from job creation that stems from higher oil prices, and the region has been through some of its own *perestroikas* in the past. I do not think real estate can go through any more adjustments. I do not think construction will have to go through any more adjustments around here, nor will the banking business. Those three areas basically have come down, stabilized and begun to move in the right direction. But they are not doing so in other parts of the country. So, I think this region has several forces going for it that the other parts of the country lack.

Long-Term Economic Outlook for the Southwest

Over the longer term, I see several factors that have the potential to boost economic growth in this region relative to the rest of the country. Among these factors are the region's proximity to Mexico and the renewed importance of the energy sector as the 1990s unfold. We also have several critical decisions to make. Two areas in which I think we are at a crossroads are educational funding and our tax structure.

Free trade with Mexico. We are in a region that probably has more to gain than other parts of the country from the free trade act that I think will eventually be passed between the United States and Mexico. A free trade act with Mexico means growth for Texas, growth for New Mexico, growth for Arizona and growth for California—the four states on Mexico's border.

Mexico is a market; it is not a menace, despite what some special interest groups may claim. Mexico lowered its protectionist wall in 1986. In the past two years, our exports to Mexico have increased by $10 billion.

Mexico means growth for Texas. When Mexico grows, the unemployment rate in Texas falls. The same is true for the other border states. The *maquiladora* industry by itself has created about 50,000 jobs in Texas alone. A U.S.–Mexico free trade agreement will only mean more of the same.

A major question on people's minds is whether a U.S.–Mexico free trade agreement means that our jobs will go south. We can debate this, but I think Jim Markusen had the right answer in his speech yesterday at this conference: there will probably be more jobs created in both countries, and both countries will benefit. Would this mean a boom for this region of the country? Probably not. Mexican tariffs have already been reduced. On average, they are lower than Canada's were at the start of U.S.–Canada negotiations. Texans already sell a great deal to Mexico, and Mexican growth has already meant some expansion here. A free trade agreement will not bring a boom, but it will mean a continuation of the underpinnings of future growth.

The real issues are whether the United States will get a free trade agreement with Mexico and, if so, when it will occur. My prediction is that it depends on whether the U.S. economy is growing or shrinking.

One lesson I have learned by observing the economy over the past 20 years is that when we experience a prolonged recession and serious unemployment, we raise our protectionist barriers in this country. It seems to have always been that way, and a prolonged recession would seriously reduce the chances for passage of a free trade agreement with Mexico. Mexico particularly is a very low-wage country in comparison with, say, Canada. And protectionist sentiment rises with the unemployment rate. So, passage of that agreement depends on continued economic gains in both the United States and Mexico. A free trade agreement is not a done deal.

Still, the potential for the proposed legislation seems great. The Bush administration seems to be 100 percent behind it. Within about two weeks, President Bush will have met with his counterpart, Mexican President Carlos Salinas, five times since they both took office. That record stands as evidence of the commitment of the leaders of both countries. If passed, the proposed legislation, together with the U.S.–Canadian free trade agreement, would create a larger market than Europe 1992, and the Southwest stands to gain disproportionately from that agreement in comparison with the rest of the nation.

Energy outlook. The long-term outlook for energy is bright, particularly in this District, because natural gas is a very important part of our energy mix. I think the long-term trend for energy prices is up, and it will be especially up around the middle of the decade.

The Dallas Fed forecast basically suggests that by the end of the decade the energy business, instead of being 10 percent of the economy of this region, will be back up to 15 percent. It will not get back up to 20 percent. But energy will be a contributor, rather than a detractor, from business in this District.

A major propelling force regarding energy, and one from which the Southwest will benefit, is concern about the environment. Concern about the environment will result in gas being favored over other forms of energy. And this region is rich in natural gas.

Chairman Alan Greenspan mentioned the 40-year time warp regarding Eastern Europe and the Soviet Union. The information is just beginning to come in about another 40-year time warp. We are seeing—through this time warp—what happens to the environment if you do not care about it, if you do not pay attention to it. From the picture that is unfolding, our environmental record is startling. Looking through a 40-year time warp shows us the changes we would fail to notice from an incremental, day-to-day perspective.

I think that the environment will be one of the key issues in the 1990s, one that will shape a growing demand for natural gas. As demand grows, gas will replace other forms of energy and the region will benefit.

Critical decisions in education and taxes. How the region comes to terms with two key issues—funding education and reforming the region's tax structure—will have a great bearing on the future.

The funding of education will force us to put our money where our mouth is. It is very easy to be the Education President, the Education Governor, and to run on that kind of ticket. It is quite another thing to be able to marshal the resources necessary to devote more resources to education. We are at the crossroads of some very key decisions on education, but the bottom line is we will have to spend more on it. But stop and look at the alternatives. Texas ranks top in the country in school dropouts, a dubious distinction that does not help attract business.

People want quality services from their governments; they demand certain services, and good quality education is one of them. And people are willing to pay for quality education. If you do not pay for it, eventually you get low incomes, slow job growth, growing crime, growing prisons and growing law enforcement costs.

The choice reminds me of the Fram oil filter commercial on TV. A car mechanic stands up with a Fram oil filter in one hand. On the floor is a broken-down engine, and the mechanic says, "Look, you can either pay me now or you can pay me later." That is what education is all about. You either pay for education now or you pay for prisons later. And we need to make some very important decisions in education that I think will be fundamental to economic growth.

Turning to taxes, we see the flip side of the political jargon we have been getting from our elected and non-elected officials recently. One of the pet phrases of the past few years has been "No new taxes, read my lips." But to reiterate, the public wants, demands and needs certain services that only the public sector can provide, and people are willing to pay for these services.

The flip side of the "no new taxes" coin is no new jails, no new schools, no road improvements, no place for the homeless, no new sewers, no clean air, and this is not an environment in which we want to live.

We must find some way to change our tax structure. One of the fallouts of the 1980s is change in our underlying economic structure. In this region, we have become heavy in the production of services relative to the production of goods. Yet, we have not changed our tax structure. I am not saying that we should tax services to the hilt. All I am saying is our economic structure—where the income comes from and the things we are spending our money on—has changed. The source of the demand has changed, the supply has changed, the economy has restructured itself. Like it or not, the economy is different from what it was at the beginning of the 1980s.

But our tax structure has not changed. And as a result, our ability to provide critical and needed public services has not changed in concomitance with our economic structure. Our tax base is running behind, and we need to explore other ways to change our tax base and to clarify our priorities. Education and the environment are two very high priorities that have received a great deal of rhetoric but very little of the funding. The same is true of infrastructure and redevelopment.

Still, we must be very careful because higher taxes do not produce economic growth, particularly with mobile industries, such as services. We need to look much more carefully at our tax structure and ways to diversify it.

Summary

The bottom line of my forecast is that the Southwest should outperform the nation, but just slightly, over the next few years. Without a windfall from special economic shocks that would favor this region, such as an oil-supply disruption, growth that exceeds the national average will be very hard to sustain. Some of the key public policy decisions to which I have alluded must be made, and those decisions need to be ones that will foster the region's long-term attractiveness.

The Future of the Texas Economy

How to educate and provide jobs for Texas' rapidly expanding working-age population was a central concern for five participants in a panel discussion at the Dallas Fed's two-day conference, "Defining the Decade."

Panelists were Dallas Fed Economist William Gruben, 1990 gubernatorial contender Tom Luce, Texas Attorney General Dan Morales, University of Texas at El Paso President Diana Natalicio and Houston Mayor Kathryn Whitmire. Michael Levy, publisher of *Texas Monthly*, moderated the two-hour discussion.

When Texans define themselves in the coming years, they must come to grips with changing demographics that will increase pressure on already strained state finances and a much-criticized educational system. These changing demographics include a working-age population that will grow more rapidly in Texas than in the nation and a birth rate that will be higher than the national average, Gruben said.

The challenge of providing an education and job opportunities for every Texan is far-reaching. In expressing ideas for meeting the challenge, panelists touched on many issues—investing in education today to become more competitive in the future, involving business in education, coping with demographic change, overcoming drug abuse and crime, restructuring the state's tax system, balancing the need for economic development and concerns about the environment, and reshaping state government. What follows are highlights of the panel's comments.

This article, written by Fiona Sigalla, Diana Palmer and Rhonda Harris, first appeared in the March/April 1991 issue of Southwest Economy, *a bimonthly publication of the Federal Reserve Bank of Dallas.*

"Pay Me Now or Pay Me Later"

Investing in education is an investment in the future. Panelists echoed this idea again and again. "Education really is the answer to what we are facing in the future," Whitmire said. "The 1990s are upon us.... We have to invest in the next century. We must begin to think now, immediately, about investing in the young people who are in our schools today."

Luce said, "The facts are that in our prison system today, nine out of 10 inmates are high school dropouts. We are not going to do anything about the drug problem and crime problem in our state until we accept that fact. That requires investment."

Morales said, "I participated not too long ago in an endeavor called the Texas Criminal Justice Summit. The governor and others wanted to round up 25 or 30 corrections and criminal justice professionals to talk about this crisis, this criminal justice crisis, this drug crisis we have in our state.

"One of the things we were doing at one of those workshops was attempting to make 10-year prison population projections," Morales continued. "We were trying to determine how many prison cells were going to be required in the next century, the year 2000. I left that particular workshop struck by the notion that when we do that, what we are doing in a very real sense is looking the 3-, 4- and 5-year-olds of today squarely in the eye and telling them essentially, 'I'm sorry. We don't have enough money to take care of you today by way of adequate or responsible levels of investment in your education, or child abuse or substance abuse treatment or prevention, or counseling services for you or your parents or guardians. We don't have enough money to take care of you today, but we are reserving you a room in 10 years. And for that room we are willing to shell out $70,000 to construct it and an additional $15,000 to $20,000 every single year in operational and administrative costs to keep you there.'"

Morales stressed the importance of an educated population in developing the economic opportunities that could provide future jobs for today's students. He said that when businesses decide where to engage in startup ventures, relocations or expansions, the factor at the top of their priority list is the availability of a technologically literate labor force.

Whitmire found other reasons to focus on education. "Every big city, every urban community in this nation is worried today about the wave of violence—the tendency of people in America to solve their problems through violence rather than through communication—and about the wave of illegal drugs and the fact that this nation is the single largest drug-consuming nation in the world.... Isn't [education] the course to opportunity for every one of the people in this nation and, therefore, shouldn't we make the best possible education available to all the children of this state?" she asked.

Natalicio said, "I would only agree with [Dallas Fed Senior Vice President] Harvey Rosenblum's comment [earlier in the conference], 'Pay me now, or pay me later.'

"From an educator's point of view, people are our most important resource, and I hope that in the years ahead all of us will begin to understand just how important a statement like that is," Natalicio said.

"Will we make the right investments?" Luce asked. The Texas economy, he said, is changing "from a natural-resource-based economy to a people-based economy. That means we must tackle [this challenge] and make the education system work."

Becoming More Competitive Through Better Education

Panelists acknowledged that the Texas Legislature is overhauling its school finance system to develop court-mandated reform but said that the state should go much further to make education a competitive advantage for Texas in the 1990s.

The state's current educational system rewards failure rather than results, Luce said, citing as an example a program that gives schools more money to put students in bilingual education and keep them there than to graduate them from bilingual education.

Quoting a 1984 audit of Texas school districts that found that 55 cents of every high school dollar went to non-academic expenditures, Luce said, "We have to get serious about the money because the public is not going to support continued 50-percent increases in spending without academic results."

In Whitmire's opinion, "We are going to have to look at the education system as a system that is run by professionals. We are going to have to set high standards and build in performance goals.... We simply will not be able to operate this single most important function of government—that of public education—with a system that says that it will treat every teacher alike, that there will be no incentive for good performance, that there will be no opportunity for any kind of merit-based compensation program or promotions based on performance. We are going to have to run our school system the way we would run a business."

Natalicio concurred, saying, "We do all kinds of merit procedures at universities, and we don't give salary increases to people who aren't being productive....I would like to urge us to give some thought to not just raising salaries, because that is just the tip of the iceberg, but also to think about the value system we have at the present time and, indeed, what we pay for in our society. We are paying for a lot of things in a lot of other professions that may not, in the long run, have the impact on our society that education will."

Luce said, "Our teacher pool today is coming from the bottom fourth of the people who go to college. We are not going to change that until we change teacher compensation." But he emphasized, "If you merely put more money in the same system, you are going to get the same results."

Luce advocated enhancing the role of principals and reducing layers of administration. "We have to have a system that lets a principal have the authority and responsibility on a school campus sufficient so you can hold that principal accountable for results. We have to have a system in which the principals can hire and fire."

Giving Business a Role in Education

Panelists urged business to become involved in changing the educational system. "What business can do in education is be the voice to demand real change," Luce said, adding, "Business can be the element that comes in and says, 'Where are the goals? Where is the action plan? How are you assessing results?'"

Whitmire added that business could give public schools both financial assistance and volunteers. "What is really working in Houston are the programs in which major corporations adopt schools in the inner city, and they not only put financial assistance into them, but they also put some volunteers into them," Whitmire said.

"They spend some time with the children in those schools. They give them exposure to the broader scope of opportunities for their future," Whitmire continued. "It is that caring about the students that makes the difference. It is the realization that solving the educational problem is part of the job of every corporate citizen in our community and every parent and volunteer. It is something that simply cannot be turned over to the bureaucracy."

How Changing Demographics Affect Educational Needs

In addition to Texas' work-force expansion and accelerating birth rate, several demographic trends will influence the future. Natalicio said that 80 percent of the state's population now live in urban areas, that the Hispanic population in Texas increased 43 percent in the past decade and that the 1990 freshman class at UTEP was 73 percent minority.

"Those are exciting demographic trends, and they add an enormous diversity to our state's population," Natalicio said, but she cautioned that these changes underscore the need to improve the participation of minority groups in education.

"Of 341 Ph.D. degrees awarded in the entire United States in 1988 in mathematics," Natalicio said, "one [recipient] was a black, two were Native American and three were Hispanic. In 1987, non-United States citizens earned twice as many doctoral degrees in all fields as minority Americans. Think about what that means in terms of our future development as a society. Those are very sobering statistics."

In El Paso today, she said, 45 percent of Hispanic youngsters and 37 percent of blacks drop out of school before they earn a high school diploma. She attributed the high minority dropout rate in part to family finances. "A lot of minority children are poor, and family finances are closely correlated with dropouts."

Improving education will mean overcoming current statistics regarding minorities and education. "This is not an issue any more of morality or of charity in dealing with minority populations; this is self-interest. If we do not begin to invest in the education of minority populations in this state—minority populations that will be the majority in this state by 2025—we will have to recognize that we have not paid the price today that our children will have to pay in the future. Our future lies in the hands of the young people who are in school today, and I hope that Texas will rise to that challenge in the 1990s," Natalicio continued.

"Unfortunately, the majority of our low-income and unstable families tend to be ethnic minorities," Whitmire said, "so you see the dropout as something that is then thought to be related to the ethnic minority status."

Whitmire argued for more preschool programs and more parental involvement to help curb the number of dropouts. Preschool programs for 3- and 4-year-olds would help the student who otherwise would start out behind, she said, explaining, "Failure in those early grades, that failure to get the appropriate learning skills, to develop the appropriate self-esteem, that brings about the dropout. If we can put the emphasis on what we are doing for the 3-year-olds and 4-year-olds to prepare them for success in school, I think we can lower the dropout rate.

"A second thing that needs to be done is more parental involvement," Whitmire continued. "There is now a belief in our community that parental involvement is very directly related to keeping the kids in school and seeing success....If we can bring more parents into the process, I believe we'll reduce the dropout rate."

Tackling Drug Abuse and Crime

Although education may be at the root of many societal problems, panelists agreed that the symptoms should not be ignored. Overcoming drug abuse and crime must be a priority, they said.

"We are going to have to tackle [these problems] at the state level, the local level, in the business community and in the education system," Whitmire said. "If we can do that, we will have better cities in which to live and better communities in which to work. And we will have economic advantages because right now we are spending an enormous amount of money through losses in the business community, losses from personal households, and an enormous amount of money on security, law enforcement, the criminal justice system and the prison system."

Luce argued for drug prevention programs in the schools. "In our schools today, we have already taken the prevention program down to the 6-year-old, down to the first-grader. We've got to go all the way down to the 3-year-old and 4-year-old....One of the saddest things in our state budget is that we allocate such a minuscule portion of what we spend on the drug problem to drug prevention," Luce said.

Whitmire proposed attacking the drug problem on four fronts: enforcement, interdiction, education and treatment. Enforcement, she said, requires "arresting the drug dealers and hopefully keeping them incarcerated a little longer than we are right now and giving them some drug treatment and rehabilitation while they are there....In addition to that is interdiction, which is primarily conducted by the federal government trying to reduce the flow of drugs into our nation by capturing more of it on the way in."

In Houston schools, Whitmire said, drug education begins in kindergarten and continues through high school. But perhaps the single biggest boost for drug education in Houston comes from enlisting the media in the effort. "They have given an enormous amount of coverage and public service attention to the drug problem," Whitmire said, "and I have to say that as hard as we work in the schools, I am afraid that people still learn more from television than from anything else. So that is why we have tried to attack this issue through the media."

Whitmire also advocated drug treatment on demand. "The fact that there are drug addicts in Texas today who would like to turn their lives around and are not able to get any kind of treatment indicates that we are not yet as serious about the problem as we ought to get about it," Whitmire said.

Luce maintained that the state must get realistic about the drug problem. "That means that in addition to building prisons, you must have a drug treatment rehabilitation program so that you can require the first-time user to have drug treatment and rehabilitation. We have got to break the cycle of drug use; if not, it will overwhelm us," he said.

Restructuring the Tax System

Texas legislators must, in the words of the state's attorney general, make a "serious and substantial effort" toward structural reformation of our tax base and our tax system to fashion a tax structure that more fairly and more accurately reflects the state's economy. Other panelists agreed.

Luce said, "We have a tax system that is taxing industries that are declining and not taxing other industries, and we are not taxing industries that are growing. I think the key element from business to support economic growth is what kind of tax system you have. Do you have a government that you can put confidence in, that you think will deal with issues with certainty, and will really solve problems, or do you have an unpredictable government that is not dealing with problems?"

Gruben tried to dispel the idea that low taxes are essential to promoting growth. "Low taxes do not necessarily mean high growth, and high taxes do not necessarily mean low growth. You have to give people what is consistent with what they want. This does not mean that people necessarily love to pay high taxes, but they are willing to pay them if they get what they want. If enough people want more education,...then they would be willing to pay those taxes, and it would not negatively or significantly affect growth. In fact, in the long term it certainly should positively affect growth.

"What this means is that the most growth-enhancing types of expenditures are the ones that should be focused on. What people do not want to pay for to a large extent is administrative costs," Gruben continued.

Morales criticized the Legislature for not utilizing all of Texas' tax base. "When it has become necessary to generate additional revenues for public purposes, the Legislature has simply taken the existing structure and raised the rates to the point where now we enjoy the second-highest general sales tax rate in the nation. We are among the top 10 states in the nation relative to the local property tax burden that Texans have had foisted on them," Morales said.

Whitmire suggested that tax reform needs to be accomplished without creating a state income tax. "The first approach needs to be directed at revamping the franchise tax rather than trying to move to an income tax. I think that may accomplish about the same thing," Whitmire said.

A state income tax may be inevitable. Morales said, "I will be surprised if we hit the next century without some form of direct income taxation somewhere in our structure....I think by the latter part of the decade the Legislature will make the determination that they have exhausted options and alternatives other than that option and find some mechanism by which to allow for the injection of some degree of profit sensitivity into our structure."

Current state tax laws, Gruben said, place Texans at a disadvantage on federal income taxes, however. "Sales taxes are no longer deductible; income tax payments for state purposes are. We do not have a state income tax, so basically we are getting burned in Washington under the current structure."

Luce emphasized that business can play a big role in the restructuring of the tax system. "Business," he said, "is going to have a golden opportunity to have an impact on public policy in Texas over this tax issue if business plays it smart. What business needs to do is be debating right now what kind of changed tax system it wants. What is a tax system that will support growth?...The tax system likely will not be changed unless business supports it or unless business is so divided it is not a factor."

Balancing Business Needs and Concern for the Environment

When it comes to balancing economic growth and environmental concerns, Luce said that business wants "predictability, certainty and reasonableness." The quality of the environment "affects the quality of life, which has an impact on who wants to move here and who wants to stay here. We have got to improve the environmental situation in the state. The key will be to do it in a way that has the predictability and certainty that business needs to grow and develop," he continued.

Natalicio said that people have been given a rather unilateral view of what the environmental issues are. "The business community is going to have to help provide information to create some sort of broader perspective within the [educational] framework to enable us to educate the population as well as we should on that issue," she said.

Morales responded, "Business in Texas has as much an interest in the development of, and ultimately the achievement of, a clean and healthful environment everywhere in our state as does any other segment of our community. I don't think we have to have one at the cost of or as a substitute for the other."

Agreeing on specific goals, in Whitmire's opinion, will be the key to dealing with environmental issues, preserving the environment and maintaining economic growth. "Once we can agree on some specific goals, then we need a plan of action to get to those goals that can be implemented on a specific timetable, which will bring about the stability and reliability that is needed for economic growth," she said.

Whitmire cited the Clean Air Act as an example of a plan with specific goals and specific timetables. "The Clean Air Act is a very big issue for this state because we are a long way from complying with national clean air standards," Whitmire said, "and we must accomplish those goals that are now set out very clearly in the federal law....They will require some changes in lifestyles, and they will require some significant investments by industry. But now that we have the goals set out and now that we have the time frame set out, our job is to define a fair and balanced plan to meet those goals. Our job is to put together a plan and meet those air quality standards."

Reshaping State Government for the 1990s

State government, Morales said, is responsible for four basic policy areas: education, corrections, transportation and human services. "If you look at how we are doing in terms of operation, administration and provision of those services and programs, I think there is significant cause for concern....In three of the four major areas of state obligation and responsibility, we are operating in this state more or less in a crisis fashion," Morales warned.

"Courts, the judiciary and judges are making what should be legislative decisions, policy decisions," Morales said. "I am hopeful that over the course of the coming years that we in state government will be successful in wresting away that policy-making discretion and authority from judges, from the judiciary, and restoring it to elected representatives, senators and others who are much better prepared and much better suited to make what are essentially legislative and political decisions.

"It simply should not be the case that in many regards we have non-elected individuals making such significant policy decisions that have such a profound and substantial impact on every Texan," Morales continued.

Luce said that voters are responsible for demanding solutions from the Legislature. "The legislative system is geared to compromise....The problem is that means we are trying to make changes on the margins, and our problems will not be solved that way. That means that you and I are going to have to be part of the chorus that demands real solutions to those problems. It is our right to vote and to participate, but we've got to be more vocal and more active in demanding real solutions," Luce argued.

Whitmire suggested that state legislators' low wages contribute to the problems in state government. "If you do a good job of [serving in the Legislature], it takes all your time and yet it doesn't pay you a living wage. So you either decide not to give it all the time you really need to or not to make a living. That is a pretty tough choice to give to the people who are making our laws."

Natalicio agreed that legislators need higher salaries, and she added that the Legislature should meet more often. "As fatiguing as it would be to have the Legislature in session on a regular basis every year, I think there is a need for a move in that direction. I also think that the issues are so complex at this point that it is essential that we provide our representatives with the kinds of salaries that will enable them to do the job in the way that we would like for them to do it."

"Special sessions now are not so special," Morales said. "In 1989, for example, the state Legislature was in session far more days than was the United

States Congress, notwithstanding the fact that Congress, of course, theoretically is a full-time legislative body. The state Legislature is part-time." Morales added that the incoming lieutenant governor has proposed to allow at least an annual budget session rather than having the Legislature attempt to anticipate spending needs and demands 24 and 30 months in advance.

Gruben asserted that there is not enough concern with performance in the state government. "State government in general is too much concerned with filling slots and allocating budgets and not enough with evaluating and monitoring performance, not only of individuals but also of agencies.

"We have problems that get by the entire system that is supposed to be handling them.... Education is one; environmental problems are another.... The usual management procedures that are now applied in the private sector don't seem to be applied with as much attention in the public sector," Gruben said.